D1366650

Nonprint in the Secondary Curriculum

NONPRINT
IN THE
SECONDARY CURRICULUM

Readings for Reference

Edited with an introduction by
James L. Thomas

1982

Libraries Unlimited, Inc.
Littleton, Colorado

LIBRARIES UNLIMITED, INC.
P.O. Box 263
Littleton, Colorado 80160

Library of Congress Cataloging in Publication Data

Main entry under title:

Nonprint in the secondary curriculum.

    Bibliography: p. 145
    1. Education, Secondary--United States--Curricula
--Addresses, essays, lectures. 2. Audio-visual
materials--United States--Addresses, essays, lectures.
I. Thomas, James L., 1945-   .
LB1628.N58   373.19   81-18596
ISBN 0-87287-274-2   AACR2

TABLE OF CONTENTS

INTRODUCTION

Educators have maintained and research has shown that individual differences among students require that teachers use a variety of media to reach the intellectual abilities of learners.[1] If we accept these findings, then it becomes clear how essential it is that all media be made available to students in the learning process.

Those of us who have had direct contact with the student of the 70s have at times perhaps been baffled, amazed, or possibly frustrated with conventional instructional approaches that for some reason did not elicit the response we have been taught to expect. As educators we have been ill-prepared to meet the needs of students who have been bombarded and overcharged with the electronic media. John Culkin, in examining this new breed of student, states that "The learner these days comes to school with a vast reservoir of vicarious experiences and loosely related facts; he is accustomed to communication through image and sound; he wants to be involved in what he is doing; he wants to use all his senses in his learning as an active agent in the process of discovery. A new learner calls for a new kind of learning."[2] If we are to reach this "new learner," then we must be willing to utilize all formats to enable our young people to discover and develop the tools necessary for survival in the 80s.

Although nonprint media is still considered by some only to supplement a print-oriented/print-dominated curriculum, more and more educators are experiencing the value of using other modes of communication to tap the individual styles of each learner. Morrow, Suid, and Suid in "Uncommon Sensing: A Model for Multi-Media Learning" have explored the design of "wheel learning," an approach that divides classroom learning into eight progressive, overlapping areas from awareness of the body to speech to design to print to photography to sound to movies to television. In their research they maintain that "Time and again, we have seen students who bring a long tradition of personal failure with print into the classroom begin to learn in a multimedia situation."[3] One of the main values they see with using such an approach is that "When a child can see print as just one member of the media family, he tends to view it more as a potential tool for communication than as a hurdle."[4]

The purpose of this particular compilation is to document the variety of ways *nonprint*, multimedia experiences have been used in the secondary setting. In reviewing the literature over the past ten years it became evident that nonprint has become more of an accepted and integral part of the school curriculum. It has been used by teachers and school library media specialists to enhance, to motivate, and to increase interest in learning across a variety of subjects. Numerous programs have also been developed in the study of nonprint in its own right, such as production of materials by students and/or visual literacy programs.

In *Nonprint in the Secondary Curriculum*, the editor has selected articles that are representative of the wide variety of ways nonprint materials have been applied to the curriculum; no other compilation to date has taken such an approach. Textbooks that have promoted the utilization, production, and study of nonprint have typically discussed each individual medium and then have attempted to show how each might apply to or be used in instruction.

This particular work includes articles written by practitioners over the past ten years and is divided into the following areas: English studies; science and foreign language; social studies and history; art and music; industrial/vocational education; production of materials in the media center and classroom; and visual literacy programs. Although the articles in the compilation are divided into specific areas, it is hoped that the reader will be able to see applications of the use or production of nonprint across the curriculum, and, as a result, be able either to replicate or to adapt the technique to his or her own subject field. Each section is preceded with a brief overview of the individual articles. An annotated bibliography for additional reading and appendices conclude the collection.

Although this compilation is a retrospective view of the last decade, most of the techniques for using and producing nonprint are still valuable and are worth emulating. Admittedly, as newer methods develop and as educational technology expands, some of these techniques will change or be replaced. However, it should be evident even to the casual reader that the widespread increase of nonprint in the curriculum during the 70s might serve as a predictor for its continued growth and acceptance during the 80s as a viable means for actively involving our young people in their own education process.

— James L. Thomas

NOTES

[1]William H. Allen, "Intellectual Abilities and Instructional Media." *A V Communication Review* (Summer 1975):139-70.

[2]John Culkin, "Education in a Post-Literate World." In *The Mediate Teacher: Seminal Essays on Creative Teaching*, selected and introduced by Frank McLaughlin. Philadelphia, PA: North American Publishing Company, 1975. p. 17.

[3]James Morrow, Murray Suid, and Roberta Suid, "Uncommon Sensing: A Model for Multi-Media Learning." In *The Mediate Teacher: Seminal Essays on Creative Teaching.* p. 36.

[4]Ibid., p. 37.

CONTRIBUTORS

CARLENE MELLO ABORN is Media Coordinator for Osceola High School in St. Petersburg Beach, Florida. "Multi-Image Productions Are Magical Motivators" is reprinted by permission of *School Library Journal* (April 1977, vol. 23, pp. 23-27), R. R. Bowker Company/A Xerox Corporation.

ROBERT K. AVERY is professor of communication, Director of Graduate Studies, Department of Communication, University of Utah, Salt Lake City. "A Rationale for the Utilization of Audio-Visual Speech Models in Teaching Speech Criticism" is reprinted by permission of *Speech Teacher* (March 1972, vol. 21, pp. 138-40).

MICHAEL L. BERGER is associate professor and Director of Teacher Education at St. Mary's College of Maryland in St. Mary's City. "The Application of Still Photography to the Teaching of History" is reprinted by permission of *Social Studies* (February 1972, vol. 63, pp. 76-79). Copyright © 1972 by Heldref Publications.

RALPH R. BUSH is a woodworking/woodcarving teacher at Pasadena High School in California. "Photo-Tape Units Put Safety First" is reprinted by permission of *School Shop* (March 1976, vol. 35, pp. 35-37) in Ann Arbor, Michigan.

DR. B. LEE COOPER is Vice President for Academic Affairs at Newberry College in Newberry, South Carolina. "Popular Music: A Creative Teaching Resource" is reprinted from *Audiovisual Instruction* (March 1979, vol. 24, pp. 37-43). Reprinted by permission of the Association for Educational Communications and Technology.

JILL C. DARDIG, Ed.D., is associate professor in the Education Department of Ohio Dominican College in Columbus, Ohio. "A Visual Literacy Program for Deaf Students" is reprinted from *Audiovisual Instruction* (October 1974, vol. 19, pp. 24-27). Reprinted by permission of the Association for Educational Communications and Technology.

DOROTHY DUNN is Grant County Librarian and elementary school librarian in Hyannis, Nebraska. "Students Shoot Their Book Reports" is reprinted from *Audiovisual Instruction* (October 1974, vol. 19, pp. 22-23). Reprinted by permission of the Association for Educational Communications and Technology.

The late PAUL F. GRIFFIN was chairman of the Department of Social Science in the Oregon College of Education in Monmouth, Oregon. "Photographs in the Classroom" is reprinted with permission of the *Journal of Geography* (May 1970, vol. 69, pp. 291-98), National Council for Geographic Education.

RICHARD GRILLOTTI is a teacher with the California Avenue School in Uniondale, New York. "Anyone Can Make a Filmstrip" is reprinted by permission of *School Arts* (December 1969, vol. 69, pp. 12-13).

KAREN HALL is an English/German teacher at Riverview Junior High School in Murray, Utah. "Turn Up Student Interest with Old Time Radio" was originally published in *Media & Methods* (February 1976, vol. 12, pp. 40-41) and is reprinted with permission.

AL HURWITZ is Coordinator of Visual and Related Arts with the Newton Public Schools in Newton, Massachusetts. "Turned-On Art" is reprinted by permission of *American Education* (March 1970, vol. 6, pp. 14-17).

LINDA KAHN is Director of Curriculum Development for Prime Time School Television, a national nonprofit educational organization that develops study materials for evening television programs. "VTR in the Classroom" was originally published in *Media & Methods* (April 1975, vol. 11, pp. 40-41) and is reprinted with permission.

JOE KAISER is Media Manager from Hampden Engineering Corporation in East Longmeadow, Massachusetts. "AV Can Be a Teacher's Biggest Help" is reprinted from the September 1977 issue of *Industrial Education* magazine with permission of the publisher. Copyright © 1977 by Macmillan Professional Magazines, Inc. All rights reserved.

BERT KEMPERS is an audiovisual consultant in the Boulder, Colorado area. "The Use of 8mm Films in Teaching Biology" is reprinted by permission of *American Biology Teacher* (March 1970, vol. 32, pp. 170-72).

DR. FRANCIS S. LESTINGI is associate professor of physics and interdisciplinary sciences at the State University College at Buffalo in New York. "Projection Pointers" is reprinted by permission of *Physics Teacher* (April 1975, vol. 13, p. 243). Copyright © 1975 by The American Association of Physics Teachers.

GORDON E. MARTIN is professor and chairman of the Industrial Arts Department at Southwest Texas State University in San Marcos, Texas. "The Industrial Arts Teacher and the Media Specialist" is reprinted from *Audiovisual Instruction* (April 1976, vol. 21, pp. 36-38). Reprinted by permission of the Association for Educational Communications and Technology.

DR. DOUGLAS K. MEYER is associate professor of geography in the Department of Geography-Geology at Eastern Illinois University in Charleston, Illinois. "The Photographic Essay in Geographic Instruction" is reprinted by permission of the *Journal of Geography* (September 1973, vol. 72, pp. 11-26), National Council for Geographic Education.

DORIS P. MILLER is an English teacher at Rutland Junior High School in Rutland, Vermont. "The Case of Filmstrip: Producing Filmstrips in the Classroom" is reprinted by permission of the *English Journal* (October

1977, vol. 66, pp. 70-72). Copyright © 1977 by the National Council of Teachers of English.

JOAN A. NEWMAN, Ph.D., is Program Administrator of Learning Resources with the Superintendent of Public Instruction in Tumwater, Washington. "Multi-Media in High School Journalism — It Really Works" is reprinted by permission of the *English Journal* (March 1972, vol. 61, pp. 381-84 +). Copyright © 1972 by the National Council of Teachers of English.

SVEIN OKSENHOLT, Ph.D., is professor of German and Norwegian with the Department of Foreign Languages and Literature at Eastern Montana College in Billings. "Put a Short-Wave Radio in Your Foreign Language Classroom" is reprinted from *Audiovisual Instruction* (May 1977, vol. 22, pp. 19-22) by permission of the Association for Educational Communications and Technology.

SAMUEL B. ROSS, JR., Ph.D., is Executive Director for Green Chimneys Children's Services and Lakeside School in New York. "Visual Literacy — A New Concept" is reprinted from *Audiovisual Instruction* (May 1972, vol. 17, pp. 12-15) by permission of the Association for Educational Communications and Technology.

MACK J. RYAN is professor emeritus of professional education at the State University of New York at Binghamton. "Slides in the Social Studies Classroom" is reprinted from *Audiovisual Instruction* (October 1978, vol. 23, pp. 32-33) by permission of the Association for Educational Communications and Technology.

EMILY SCOTT is vice president and assistant manager for Michigan Blind Sales in Detroit, Michigan. She has published numerous articles on art education and lectures to teachers' groups and civic organizations. "The Hand-Made Slide: Whetstone for Perceptual Acuity" is reprinted by permission of *Arts and Activities* (April 1972, vol. 71, pp. 30-31).

CHARLES B. TAYLOR, Ph.D., teaches creative writing in various schools around Texas and elsewhere as part of the artist-in-the-schools program of the National Endowment for the Arts. "To Videotape or Not To Videotape ... " is reprinted from *Audiovisual Instruction* (January 1977 supplement, vol. 22, pp. 33-34 +) by permission of the Association for Educational Communications and Technology.

BUFORD L. WILLIAMS is a physics teacher at Kimball County High School in Kimball, Nebraska. "Projecting Polaroid Photographs" is reprinted by permission of *Science Teacher* (March 1974, vol. 41, p. 41).

DR. FRANK M. YOUNG is currently teaching at Minneapolis College of Art and Design, Visual Studies, and Product Design and has his own design firm, White Line Design in Lake Crystal, Minnesota. "Visual Literacy Today and Tomorrow" is reprinted by permission of *Arts & Activities* (February 1973, vol. 73, pp. 44-45).

DR. RUTH ZINAR is associate professor of music education with York College of City University of New York. "Using Visual Media in Music Instruction" originally appeared in *American Music Teacher* (April 1979, vol. 28, pp. 20, 22) and is used by permission.

ENGLISH STUDIES

English studies on the secondary level incorporate a variety of areas of major importance to the curriculum and to the language acquisition by the student: the development of writing skills, the study of the literatures of different countries, drama, and public speaking. The use of nonprint has been used by professionals to enhance and expand typically print-oriented approaches. The results are evident as seen in the articles included in this section.

Dorothy Dunn in "Students Shoot Their Book Reports" uses videotaping to put the spark back in a semester-fatigued classroom. She explains in detail the organization necessary for a meaningful first encounter with television production from group selection to script writing to planning backgrounds and graphics to actual filming. Charles B. Taylor describes in "To Videotape or Not To Videotape ... " his reasons for allowing his students also to use video. He relates his rationale for utilizing this format in place of the traditional term paper requirement on Shakespeare and the benefits realized by the students in experimenting with this medium.

In contrast to the use of a visual medium, Karen Hall sees the benefits derived from a purely auditory medium — radio. In "Turn Up Student Interest with Old-Time Radio," the author demonstrates her belief in the value of improving listening skills, sharpening imagination, and heightening involvement to be derived from students tuning in to old-time radio or from writing their own original scripts for taping and sharing with other classes. Joan A. Newman in "Multi-Media in High School Journalism — It Really Works" also employs radio broadcasting along with newsfilm and photography. With the increased costs of printing and the decreased student interest in a typical journalism class, Ms. Newman shows how she turned this situation around by experimenting with the capabilities of nonprint as a viable means for improving the communication skills and increasing enthusiasm in journalism.

The last article in this section, by Robert K. Avery and entitled "A Rationale for the Utilization of Audio-Visual Speech Models in Teaching Speech Criticism," is a strong statement regarding the importance of having the combined visual and auditory media, either 16mm film or videotape, available for students taking speech courses. Avery admits to the immediate availability of most speeches in a printed format, but he feels that more is to be gained by the student able to both watch and listen to the actual presentation.

STUDENTS SHOOT THEIR
BOOK REPORTS

Dorothy Dunn

The shock of recognition! There I was, staring glassy eyed at the eighth grade English class, and they were looking blankly back at me. We both knew we suffered from near-end-of-semester dulldrums. No antagonism, just a realization that things had gone completely blah.

So I tossed the book on my desk and wandered across the room trying to think of a vital something to revive a learning atmosphere. Just as I reached the TV set, someone droned out, "Book reports again?"

Oh, oh, there was a straw to grasp at. "Look, kids, you have enjoyed the John Robbins 'Matter of Fiction' series. Now how would you like to do a similar thing for your book reports?"

A few heads turned as questioning eyes sought questioning eyes. "Whatta ya mean?"

"Well, you could divide into groups and choose a book you would all read. Then you would write a script, learn to operate the videorecorder and film your presentation for a book report."

A few questions, and then a vote, with three-quarters of the class affirmative to giving the idea a try. A time limit of three days was given in which the groups were to select a book. The next 10 days were for reading the books. Before the unit started, each pupil handed me a slip with names of persons he or she would prefer to work with; and, using these, I drew up groups of four which I posted the next morning.

By the deadline for reading, I had managed to produce enough materials to get started. I also had looked through the few "Matter of Fiction" tapes I still had on hand and selected the ones I wanted for demonstration purposes.

The first ditto sheet handed to the kids contained the three broad objectives; briefly, to identify a suitable book for dramatization, to write a script using book incidents, to film the book presentation. It also listed formalities to be observed, such as titling the show, appointing a group member to be a narrator, one to be cameraman, one to be VTR operator, and one to serve as propman. The respective duties and responsibilities were outlined.

On a second sheet I had broken the unit into four main areas with a suggested number of days, objectives, and activities. The first four-day period was for critical viewing, during which the kids would watch reruns of "Matter of Fiction" shows, this time paying attention to background music, titles and credits, show openings, show structuring and endings.

Pupils were given check sheets to use while viewing. The sheets listed items to look for. We reran scenes as many times as comments indicated we needed to,

Reprinted by permission of the author and the Association for Educational Communications and Technology from *Audiovisual Instruction* 19 (October 1974):22-23.

and students began to get a little more sophisticated about factors going into show production. We examined how a mood might be set; how a camera might be far off for an opening scene and then dollied in for a close up, or the reverse; how the camera might shoot through a frame; how artwork might introduce setting or characters; how the story might be carried by narrative summaries or reenacted while actual paragraphs from the book were read; how props were introduced and used. The class decidedly did not care for a chorus of voices, and they quickly noted that music lowered in volume or ceased when a voice was speaking. They were delighted by funny scenes with quick, up-beat music. And they especially liked an ending that had barn doors closing which neatly symbolized the ending.

Five days had been allotted for script writing, and another five for planning backgrounds and graphics. Four final days were set aside for learning the technical features of production.

Script writing was by far the least popular activity. The groups were to decide what scenes in their book they wanted to feature, then assign each member to write a portion of the script. With the narrative outlined, they were to fit in visuals and, lastly, to fill in directions for the cameraman. One team had a dominant member who wanted to do the entire script her way by herself; a group of boys tried to argue that the narrator ought to write the script; and none of the groups really planned well enough for smooth transitions between scenes. However, we were lucky in getting some high school volunteers to type the scripts so the narrator had legible copy to work with for the filming.

The graphics production unit was attacked enthusiastically. The camera was brought in, and two pieces of student artwork were shown on the monitor. The class quickly saw what was meant by correct dimensional proportion, and that bold dark lines made the best pictures. Illustrations from books were roughed out on transparency film and then projected by overhead projector onto large pieces of tag board and traced. Some talented students produced their own drawings, and the art teacher was persuaded to do some sketches for a group. Another group planned to use a sheet for a backdrop, and made transparencies to be thrown from behind for various background scenes. Stencils were traded frantically as credit cards were made. These were busy, noisy, productive days.

Once cameramen and VTR operators were chosen, they were given a self-teaching sheet and "hands on" experience until they knew the routines. Before they could shoot, however, they had to pass an operator's test.

The actual filming was, of course, the highlight. The groups signed up for after school or after supper use of the studio (classroom)—a hardship since almost all of our kids are bussed in from ranches. Parents had to make a special trip.

Getting ready averaged an hour and a half as props were maneuvered into suitable locations, graphics hastily finished, lighting tested, and sequences run through to familiarize everyone with what he or she was to do when. Each show was filmed about half way through, then stopped and the footage shown to the cast. This gave everyone relief from the harum scarum of preparations and provided a settling down period. Mistakes were discovered and laughed at, improvements suggested, and resolves made to get it right for the final filming. The shows in the can averaged about 12 minutes.

All groups experienced disillusionment and hilarity during the filming. They also gained respect for a professional show. All were ready to admit weaknesses in preparation that showed up during production, but all could see good things happening, too. There were no real failures.

The finished shows were run for two consecutive class periods, with each person filling out an evaluation sheet on each show. Discussions were quite realistic, and the kids readily admitted what needed improvement while also complementing the superior portions. They agreed that the project had been worthwhile, and that they had learned a lot. They felt sure they would want to try again sometime. Best of all, the dulldrums had been scuttled!

Since not all teachers of English have a media background, media persons might just win a few points by suggesting a project such as ours to a local teacher and helping with the technical aspects. The kids will thank you, too.

TO VIDEOTAPE OR
NOT TO VIDEOTAPE . . .

Charles B. Taylor

An essential point, continually stressed by teachers of literature, is that the great English poet Shakespeare is first and foremost a playwright. His plays were written for performance on the stage in front of a live audience, and not for study in the classroom from a printed text. Shakespeare, unlike a novelist, leaves much up to the visual apprehension of the audience—matters such as scenery, costumes, character "appearance" (which includes gesture, voice tone, movement, etc.).

A novelist will describe a room or a character's position and movement in a room, and will tell you, often in great detail, what the character actually looks like. A theater audience, in contrast, actually sees these things and therefore a play is written in a much different manner than a novel.

An audience approaches a play in a different mood than a reader approaches a novel. Shakespeare's Elizabethan audience was an active bunch—a potpourri of apprentices, prostitutes, country folk in London for a night on the town, and highly sophisticated aristocrats. They came to the theater to be entertained and to have their emotions engaged—a different experience from that of the solitary reader who approaches a novel in a usually more reflective and quiet mood.

Even though these points are stressed by the knowledgeable teacher, as the course proceeds, you'll find that class discussions still seem to center on the text, on the printed word before the student's eyes. A major difficulty is how to overcome the conflict between what we as teachers would like to do with drama and what we can actually do in practice within the confines of the classroom.

One commonly used method to bring practice and theory closer together is to show film versions of Shakespeare's plays during class. Many fine, if somewhat dated, film productions are available. Charles W. Eckert's book *Shakespearean Films* (Prentice-Hall, 1972) is a helpful text that contains reviews of many of the classic Shakespeare films and a bibliography of Shakespeare films in numerous languages.

Although the film version of the plays gives the students some idea of the *visual* aspects of a play, it does not provide any *experienced* knowledge of how plays are made or put together and thus different from other forms of literature. It is for this reason that I use videotape equipment in the teaching of Shakespeare to complement both the showing of films and the close reading of the text.

I present the use of videotape as a project that students may do in place of the traditional term paper. I point out that writing criticism, locating articles for quotation, and studying the text of Shakespeare is a worthwhile endeavor. Through such concentrated study they can learn how to do research in literary studies as well as learn a lot about one small aspect of Shakespeare. I also point

Reprinted by permission of the author and the Association for Educational Communications and Technology from *Audiovisual Instruction* 22 (January 1977 supplement):33-34 + .

out, however, that research on Shakespeare is a veritable industry in itself. In order for students to shed any new light on a Shakespeare topic, they will need to read a good deal of criticism, be highly imaginative, and select a limited topic. While a text-centered investigation will provide insights into the themes and poetic techniques of the play, working with videotape will give them an experiential understanding of the sounds of dramatic poetry and how Shakespeare handled action, scene and character interactions.

During the first week, the students decide what kind of a project they want to do. Usually about half the class—ten to 15 students—choose to go with the videotape. A common time is found when they can all get together to learn how to use the videotape equipment. I have the students sign a written mimeo "contract" to help protect the production company against sudden drop-outs. Of course, there is no way to stop a student from leaving the group, but the contract does force them to review their schedule to see if they can afford the time and make a psychological commitment to the production.

At the first common meeting of the company, the instructor shows the students the equipment and explains how it is used. Each student then experiments with it, holding the camera and pointing it at someone to record an image. Once they have become comfortable with the equipment, decisions then need to be made as to what each student's function will be in the company. You will need a director, a camera person, and a sound/prop person, as well as numerous actors. Students can go through their wardrobes looking for clothes which look Elizabethan, or Roman (for such plays as *Julius Caesar* or *Coriolanus*), or they can pick clothes for costumes which are somewhat neutral in appearance. For special effect, they may wish to use modern clothes, such as in Burton's *Hamlet*. Another option is to try to borrow from the costume departments in the drama school.

Next, the production company needs to get together and choose scenes for videotaping. Such a decision will be a tough one to make, and requires some help from the teacher who has a wide-ranging familiarity with the plays. Of course, you want the students to be able to choose a scene they find interesting and exciting. Yet, here is where they begin to get a feeling for the practical aspects of theater. They will need to find a scene which can be handled, given the limitations of the company. How many male parts are there in the scene? How many female parts? Does one character dominate the scene, leaving the other members of the company with little to do? I encourage the students to shoot "on location"—to find houses that resemble castles like MacBeth's Dunsinore; interiors that look like a royal Danish palace, etc. In one production from *Hamlet*, a local park was used to shoot the drowned Ophelia floating dead amongst lily pads; a Baptist church was used to suggest her unofficial burial service; and a local cemetery provided a freshly dug grave for the gravedigger scene. The students even borrowed skulls and bones from the biology department for the old gravedigger to toss out.

Once tasks and acting roles have been chosen and scenes decided, scripts will be needed. Dates for a first rehearsal need to be set, when all actors should have all their lines memorized. I allow two weeks. Meanwhile, the camera and sound people can be thinking about locations to videotape, and the prop person can be working on costumes. The first rehearsal can be held in a classroom. My practice is to attend this rehearsal only. I help the actors and director in understanding the scene and individual lines, give the director "tips" on how to coach actors and draw out a good performance. After this visit, I let them go on their own, but not without setting dates for rehearsals on location. The camera person, sound person, and prop person attend this first rehearsal and make reports to the company on what they have worked out.

The students then rehearse in costume "on location." The camera person and sound person work out camera angles (making notes in a logbook) and solve sound problems (is there a distracting background noise from traffic; are the microphones close enough to the actors?). These rehearsals can be videotaped and viewed through the camera itself by the company while on "location." That is the beauty of videotape—instant replay. There is no delay in sending the tape to be developed, and unlike film, it can be used over and over.

When the company is finally satisfied with their videotape, it is then shown to the class for comments, questions, suggestions. I make the final determination with regard to grades, however. To do this, I view the videotape numerous times to see how each individual did his or her part. Often, students in the company get different grades. I do point out, however, that one person not doing the job right might pull down the grade of the entire group.

So now the task is concluded. Hopefully, the students have learned a great deal about Shakespeare and drama in the process of this experience— how scenes are structured, how action and character are developed, how poetic dialogue works and is read, and how the plays of Shakespeare were, in a sense, the works of many. Shakespeare's genius, in part, stems from the poet being experienced in acting, directing, and theater ownership. The students really sense this fact after forming a company and working together to make videotaped scenes from Shakespeare.

TURN UP STUDENT INTEREST
WITH OLD-TIME RADIO
Karen Hall

Old-time radio is a refreshing and stimulating medium that can add enjoy-ment and interest to the daily classroom routine while providing an intellectual experience that is painless to the average student.

In my own use of old-time radio, I have found that students' listening skills are renewed and sharpened, imaginative and creative skills expanded, involve-ment heightened. The materials are readily available, and the programs lend themselves to any classroom situation or age group. The subject matter is flexible enough that the teacher can use smatterings of it throughout many units or design a specific unit to cover old-time radio alone.

The buzz of excitement that is the end product of using old-time radio sometimes is slow in starting. We have become a nation of lookers, not listeners. For most young people, radio is a background medium; the idea of just *listening* can bring on a case of the fidgets. But "just listening" is an important skill — as any teacher who has repeated directions five or six times can attest. And radio is a most effective "just listening" medium.

The first step, then, might be to use old-time radio to help students reju-venate their atrophied listening skills. This could be done through simple memory exercises, asking them to recall particular details of the radio program. If the students themselves make up the questions, they are honing their listening skills even as they devise questions to develop these same skills — a neat double-barrelled approach.

Not only are listening skills revitalized by exposure to old-time radio, but creative and imaginative skills are also stimulated. Today we are used to having all the blanks filled in for us. We know exactly what Pepper Anderson, Fred San-ford, and Archie Bunker look like. But what about Fibber McGee, Colonel Lemuel Q. Stoopnagle, Helen Trent, Kay Kyser, Ma Perkins, Lum and Abner, Henry Aldrich? What does the town of Pine Ridge, Arkansas, look like? Students could write a descriptive paragraph on a radio character or setting. They might type-cast people they think best fit the image of Senator Claghorn, Titus Moody, or Mrs. Nussbaum. They could listen to part of "Grand Central Station" and then guess how it will end. The possibilities are limitless.

For a more ambitious class project, students could create their own radio program. There are many types from which to choose: comedy, soap opera, science fiction, western, adventure, drama. All have old-time prototypes that can serve as guides for modern day re-creations. And the project lends itself to a unique experience that heightens student involvement in the classroom. The class writers can author the play. The academically or historically inclined can research the event or era to be portrayed. The talkers, clowns, actors, and actresses can assume the character roles. The mechanically oriented students become the

Reprinted by permission of *Media and Methods* 12 (February 1976):40-41.

recording technicians. Those with artistic inclinations might create the atmosphere of the old-time radio studio in the classroom. Others could be responsible for sound effects, a major aspect of radio broadcasting. In short, even the most lackadaisical student can get involved in the project, and all the students will gain and grow from adding something to the experience. Once the program is on tape, it can be replayed for other classes. Students enjoy hearing something that their peers put together, and the credits provide a well-earned recognition for the originators of the program.

Any teacher with a few free minutes for creative thought can come up with numerous activities for student involvement through old-time radio. Foreign language teachers might adapt the medium to their specific language. History teachers can recreate past events through radio plays. Again, all are involved and all learn. Math teachers might adapt the format of the old *Quiz Kids* show. Elementary classes can use *Let's Pretend* as a springboard for introducing old-time radio to the students. All it takes is a little imagination, a little initiation, and some carefully chosen programs. The class will usually take it from there.

The possibilities and uses of old-time radio are as varied and numerous as there are teachers and students willing to investigate. Many old programs like *Lux Radio Theatre* and *Mercury Theatre of the Air* have adapted literary works that would enrich any English class. Sociology and psychology classes could use Orson Welles' rendition of *War of the Worlds* as a prime example of mass hysteria and individual response to fear. What made Americans panic as they did? Let the students listen to the original broadcast and see what they think. Fill them in on the historical atmosphere of the time, and a learning experience about themselves and human nature can take place.

Old-time radio is a cornucopia of past events, trends, and insights. Listening to it can be informative and enjoyable for students and teachers. Whether it is to develop more precise listening skills, to increase the opportunities for creative expression, or to foster a deeper awareness of the human condition, there are few invitations that can compare with the stirring call to "Return with us now to those thrilling days of yesteryear ... "

Old-Time Radio Resources

Records and Tapes

For catalogs listing subjects and prices, write the following dealers:

Remember Radio, Inc.
P.O. Box 2513
Norman, OK 73069

The Radio Store
Box 203
Oradell, NJ 07649

The Radio Vault
Box 9032
Wyoming, MI 49509

Sights and Sounds of America, Inc.
Box 616
Nassau, DE 19969

Audio Antiques
Box 665
Cleveland, OH 44101

Radio Memories
1033 Gypsum
Salina, KA 67401

Radio Reruns
Box 724
Redmond, WA 92052

McCoy's Recording, Inc.
P.O. Box 1069
Richland, WA 99352

The Hall Closet
Box 421
Morton Grove, IL 60053

National Recording Co.
P.O. Box 395
Glenview, IL 60025

Radiola (for records only)
Radio Yesterday (for tapes)
Box H
Croton-on-Hudson, NY 10520

Books

In addition to the books listed below, public libraries and local bookstores should be consulted for further resources.

The Big Broadcast, 1920-1950 by Frank Buxton and Bill Owen (Avon, $3.95)

Jim Harmon's Nostalgia Catalogue by Jim Harmon (Hawthorne Books, $4.95)

Panic Broadcast by Howard Koch (Avon, 95¢)

A Pictorial History of Radio by Irving Settel (Grosset and Dunlap, $9.95)

Radio! by G. Howard Poteet (Pflaum, $3.95)

Remember Radio by Ron Lackman (G. P. Putnam's Sons, $6.95)

MULTI-MEDIA IN HIGH SCHOOL
JOURNALISM – IT REALLY WORKS   Joan A. Newman

The multi-media approach to journalism at Redmond, Washignton, High School has stimulated new enthusiasm from our students, more reactions from their audience, and new growth for the program, all at no extra cost. Our journalism staff produces a newspaper, a newsfilm, and an in-school radio broadcast, as well as doing the darkroom work in black-and-white photography for the paper and the yearbook. The two years we have experimented with the program have convinced us that the multi-media approach is a really workable method for teaching journalism.

We turned to media other than our school newspaper in 1969-70 because printing costs were rising and enrollment in our journalism course was sagging. In the five years since Redmond High School had opened, the cost of printing a four-page paper had risen from $115 to $175, though the annual budget we were allowed had remained fixed at $2500. At $300, the cost of one eight-page issue would have been more than the budget for a whole month.

Furthermore, although the student body had grown from about 1000 to 1450, enrollment in the only journalism class had remained at twenty to twenty-five. An introductory journalism class never had attracted a large enough enrollment to justify keeping it in the curriculum. For instance, one semester nine students had enrolled in the introductory class; another semester a very small introductory journalism group had been rounded out with students who needed an English class to graduate but had no particular interest in journalism.

The school principal was concerned that a disproportionate share of the school budget went to a course that was not growing as the student body expanded. Yet if we had attracted more students to the program, we could not have afforded to publish their efforts anyway.

A film criticism course at Redmond was already drawing an enrollment of 350, so we knew student interest in film was high. We knew that about fifteen minutes of Super-8 film cost a total of $20. Students could make eight fifteen-minute films of school events for the cost of one four-page paper. We decided to try film as a news medium and offered newsfilm production as an elective in the journalism program.

The idea worked! The first year the staff alternated one eight-page newspaper, the *Blaze*, with a twelve- to twenty-five minute *Blaze Newsfilm* each month. Halfway through the year, our principal and the district administration obtained for us a state-Federal grant of $600. We were then able to purchase a Super-8 camera, a Super-8 projector, and editing equipment to replace that which students had brought from home to use. (We also bought a reserve supply of film

Reprinted by permission of the author and the National Council of Teachers of English from *English Journal* 61 (march 1972):381-84+ .

that we still use for special projects and to keep the program going until regular supplies arrive each fall.)

Newsfilms were shown to the student body in our little theater or on the cafetorium stage during all study periods on show dates. We estimated the audience on any given day at about eight hundred. Content included everything from impromptu snowball fights, visual explorations of the school roofs and storage rooms, and the "Car of the Lot" in action, to gymnastics meets and cross-country practices, the all-school Environment Day, and the girls in the woodshop program. Periodically, students produced reruns for smaller groups who might have missed the original showing or were anxious to see themselves again in a particular sequence.

At the start of the following year, enthusiastic journalism students requested an additional elective, the inschool broadcast. The *Blaze Radio*, as they called it, was incorporated into the program. This project ran into considerable difficulty with equipment, all student-owned except for the school tape recorders. Nevertheless, the broadcast staff put together a bi-weekly program of interviews, sports reports, some spot news, editorials and music commentary, interspersed with "commercials" advertising school events.

Midway through the year, the student body officers all resigned their positions, saying they were unable to accomplish their goals regarding such things as the school dance policy and student desire for open campus because they had no power. The next *Blaze Radio* broadcast included interviews with students and faculty who were asked whether or not they thought the student body officers had been justified in quitting in the middle of the year.

In other broadcasts, editorials covered that question and broader topics such as mass media responsibilities and ethical questions about scholarships offered by groups which discriminate against blacks. In one broadcast feature, two students spoofed educational jargon: "Do you know what a 'building leader' is, Ed?" Another feature took students on a tour of the tunnels underneath the school: "Hey, John, what is this thing, now? (Clank, clank)." A third feature was a visit with the cooks who answered questions about their work schedule and the sources of their recipes. One local business firm actually bought two spots to advertise records. These broadcasts were aired every other Friday during study periods in the cafetorium.

In 1970-71, the staff produced a bi-weekly, four-page newspaper alternating with the broadcasts. The fifteen-minute newsfilms ran on a three-week production schedule. Our budget remained the same, since the broadcasts cost nothing.

During both these years, we found it a good idea to keep the *Blaze* newspaper publishing as much as possible because many of the students still felt most at home working with the print media (newspaper and yearbook). We also retained and expanded somewhat the work the students could do in photography, which some students felt was very important to them. With a larger darkroom we could have accommodated even more students. In fact, the darkroom was one area in which our costs did rise slightly — about $50 for supplies. However, since most of the additional work done in the darkroom was used in the yearbook, that budget absorbed the increase. Students did their own camera work, developing, and printing for just about all the black-and-white photographs in the yearbook. They also did all the photography for the paper and screened the prints for offset reproduction.

By 1971 students could elect to work in any of the four media. Many of them worked in two, some in all four. There was no clear pattern in their choices, except that those who did well in one area seemed anxious to try all the others. At the end of the year, the school acquired a videotape recorder. Some journalism students made plans to videotape and broadcast interviews with the student body and panel discussions of student concerns.

What gains in the teaching of journalism resulted from all this activity? Enrollment in the class jumped from thirty to ninety-four in the two years. These figures include the yearbook staff, which grew from nine to twenty-four in a kind of corollary action. The yearbook was transferred to journalism from the art program in the second year of the multi-media experiment. We assume that either the chance to work in photography or the general shot-in-the-arm given the journalism program by the new approach was responsible. A number of yearbook staff members tried their hand at work on the broadcast and newspaper also.

About 85 per cent of the students' work was used in one medium or another. Some material was channeled into the local weeklies as press releases from the school, but students preferred to see their work in the *Blaze*. From time to time, material originally intended for the newspaper was shortened and used for broadcast instead. One casualty with the larger staff was the use of editorials written by students not on the journalism staff. This situation was unfortunate because the *Blaze* editorial page had drawn students not on the staff into some pretty lively forums in previous years. The content of Redmond journalism now became more exclusively the project of just those students who were able to take the course.

However, we were certainly able to teach many more kinds of students than before. Traditionally, we had enrolled all comers who gave a coherent reason for wanting to take the course, but we had warned applicants that they should have "B or better" grades in English or they might not do well in journalism. Now writing skill was no longer the chief requirement for success, although the ability to organize was still highly important. We could now work with students who could organize by methods other than writing. We could also give more attention to other important communications skills, such as the ability to interview other people successfully, the ability to judge an audience, and the ability to sense how a subject will come across on movie film or in a black-and-white print.

One of the first things we did with a story possibility was to determine whether it could be told best in print, on movie film, in a broadcast, or in a single photograph or series of photographs. At that point the story was assigned to a volunteer working in the medium the staff had selected. Soon, students in editorial or management positions led their own staffs in making these decisions for themselves. They learned the advantages of the four media. They also learned to tell what parts of the same story would have greater effect in one medium than in another.

One such story was the controversy over admitting girls to the Lettermen's Club. The story was covered in the usual way in the news and editorial columns of the *Blaze*. The *Blaze Radio* collected on tape and then broadcast a cross-section of student and faculty opinion on the matter. *Blaze* photographers made pictures of the major personalities in the controversy. The newsfilm contained sequences showing the girls' athletic teams in action while the sound track explained that these were the girls who were asking to be admitted to the all-male club.

The students enjoyed making these decisions. The teacher was able to use this enthusiasm to advantage in teaching them to communicate responsibly. When it came to deciding how a story should be treated, no one said, "Oh, but that's so dull!" in those two years. If anything, students (rather than the teacher) became conscious of possible reactions from authorities and other students.

Reactions from students and faculty kept them alert to the effect their work was having on their audience. The more difference there was between what the staff thought they had said and what their audience heard or saw, the more the staff members learned.

On one occasion, broadcast staff members decided to treat a schoolwide grumble about losing basketball games by asking a haphazard sample of students and faculty, "What do you think should be done to improve school sports?" When one interviewer asked this question of a coach, he was told that his question was inflammatory and broadcasting the answers wouldn't do any good anyway. No one else had to explain to the student that rewording the question was necessary if he was going to get the kind of information he was looking for.

The students who wrote an editorial series on student conduct in the *Blaze*, called "Dick and Jane at Mickey Mouse High," learned the same lesson a different way. They attacked lunch line panhandlers and especially the "Weedies for Lunch Bunch." Their work was reprinted in two other Washington school papers as well as being quoted on our own campus. Their success taught them very efficiently how to reach at least one kind of audience with at least one message they felt was important.

There have been, of course, some drawbacks to the multi-media approach, at least as we have used it. We found it difficult to organize the program at first. It has been important to the students in our program for each one to be able to choose his own medium. It has also been important to them to be able to change to another medium or to add another to their repertoires. But it is hard to keep to a production schedule with an unstable staff. Fortunately, the printers are the only people outside the school to whom we are responsible for keeping to production schedules. If enrollment in the course stabilizes in the future, perhaps advanced students will settle into managing positions in the separate media and solve the problem.

It has also been difficult in this program to supervise all the production steps, since so many projects are in the works at once. To overcome this problem, we are thinking of using team-teaching approaches with the different media. The broadcast, for instance, could be supervised by a speech-journalism-electronics teaching team. Another possibility is using paraprofessionals, or "teacher aides," to help students with specific techniques, once the techniques have been explained by the teacher.

A third interesting possibility is using individualized instruction materials such as short films, filmstrips, charts, and tapes which explain the separate steps for producing stories in each of the media. Students could use any of these on their own to review or reinforce their understanding of specific techniques, at the time when they needed to use them.

This year, one of our advanced journalism students made a short film accompanied by a sound tape which explained the proper ways to film a moving subject. Another planned a similar lesson to demonstrate the proper use of panning with a movie camera. The teacher made a filmstrip with a sound tape to accompany it, designed to help a student write an effective headline. These are only secondary materials, of course, but using them could take much pressure off the publications advisor.

The drawbacks of the multi-media journalism program we have been working with at Redmond can certainly be overcome. The potential is great for teaching students to communicate effectively. Of course, our program is very young and many possibilities for improving it will have to be explored. But already, we have found, it really works!

A RATIONALE FOR THE UTILIZATION
OF AUDIO-VISUAL SPEECH MODELS
IN TEACHING SPEECH CRITICISM

Robert K. Avery

Just as the training of critical audiences has been considered a fundamental objective in the basic speech course for some time, the use of speech models as a pedagogical technique is rooted in classical rhetoric. Frandsen[1] and Jabusch[2] have traced the uses of speech models from the sophists of ancient Greece to their inclusion in modern speech instruction. Matlon[3] reports that from a total of 1396 speech instructors responding to his questionnaire survey, 865 made use of speech models in their basic speech course. Of those who did not employ models, many indicated that lack of time was the primary factor for not using them. Although the reasons given for utilizing the models are numerous, the main purpose was to "illustrate the principles of public speaking."[4]

In an earlier article, Baird stated that the use of models in the speech classroom should help the students to "improve in communicative technique, ability in criticism, understanding of the theory of communication and appreciation of public address as a force in history and in contemporary society."[5] Finding agreement with the second purpose mentioned by Baird was a respondent to Matlon's questionnaire, who, in discussing his use of speech models explained, "All our students ought to be prepared to function as knowledgeable critics of the public speaking they hear."[6] Ridgeway had previously supported this position when stating, "In order that pupils may be put on guard against swallowing whole everything which they read or hear, the teacher may use a systematic study and evaluation of examples."[7]

It if is accepted that examples of oral discourse might well contribute to the acquisition of critical skills, the instructor's task becomes one of selecting the models that provide for the most effective learning experience. Wilson and Arnold[8] contend that the closer the reproduction approximates the actual speaking event, the more it contributes to the accuracy of the critic's evaluations. They submit that a sound motion picture of the speech would be the next best thing to actually being there. Cathcart concurs with this position: "The best copy of a speech would be a motion picture or a video tape with a sound track. This would be as faithful a reproduction of the total speech as one could hope to obtain. Next best would be a tape recording of the voice of the speaker, including the reactions of the audience as the speech was presented."[9] Since an audio-visual reproduction provides a critic with vital information not contained within a printed transcript of the speech, it would seem logical to assume that relying solely upon speech manuscripts as instructional models, deprives students of relevant stimuli that will later influence their evaluative judgments of speakers both in and out of the speech classroom. Yet, Matlon's findings point out that in teaching students to

Reprinted by permission of the author and *Speech Teacher* 21 (March 1972):138-40.

properly evaluate past speeches, instructors used printed speeches contained in textbooks and speech anthologies as their major source of instructional models.[10]

It is commonly agreed that the "meanings" assigned by an auditor to the aural and visual components of a live oral presentation are not the same as the meanings a reader of an accurate transcript of the same speech would attribute to the printed message. Auditory and visual cues help the listener attach meanings to the verbal symbols which are similar to the meanings intended by the speaker. As Harrison[11] explains, " ... multi-band presentations provide a channel for metacommunication. As one band provides information, another band provides instructions for interpretation: 'This is important, this is rewarding, this is for you.' "

The importance of nonverbal communication has been expressed by numerous writers in recent years. Despite the variety of specific interests represented by these writers, they would probably all agree that the contributions made by nonverbal cues to the final message derived from the total communications setting, occasionally outweigh those of the verbal content. Applied to the basic speech course, their observations would seem to encourage instructors to educate students to be aware not only of what they are communicating to others through nonverbal cues, but to learn to identify nonverbal cues in the behavior of others. Stated more specifically in terms of developing critical skills, the instructor should provide students with the opportunity to study the "nonverbal content" of speech models. Thus, as noted above, if exposure to these visual and auditory cues during a student's initial speech training contributes to the development of critical skills, the inclusion of audio-visual speech models as an integral part of the instruction received should minimize the time required to achieve criterion performance. That is, the number of speeches the learner would need to critique before demonstrating acceptable skills as a speech critic should be reduced. Furthermore, with a trend toward increased use of individualized instruction practices, the possible utilization of audio-visual speech models for self-instruction cannot be overlooked. In an individualized learning situation, the presentation of a variety of filmed or videotaped speech models would thus serve to illustrate rhetorical principles as well as provide the additional critiquing experience currently afforded by fellow student speakers.

Due to the immediate availability of printed materials, many instructors apparently have been willing to sacrifice the aural and visual features of the rhetorical event and settle for the "residual message" that appears upon the printed page. Although educators may well have been justified in making this decision five or ten years ago, the present availability of low cost videotape equipment in an ever-growing number of speech departments makes audio-visual presentations almost as accessible for classroom use as printed materials. Much of the equipment currently on the market permits instructors to record televised speeches, press conferences, etc., in addition to the recording and playback of local "live" performances. In short, inexpensive hardware has reached a degree of sophistication that puts easily accessible audio-visual speech models into the hands of nearly every instructor who desires to take the trouble to use them.

Notes

[1]Kenneth D. Frandsen, "The Effects of Speech Models on Changes in Behavior in an Introductory College Course in Speech," Unpublished Ph.D. dissertation (Ohio University, 1962).

²David M. Jabusch, "An Experimental Comparison of the Lecture-Discussion and Lecture-Demonstration Methods of Teaching the Basic College Course in Public Speaking," Unpublished Ph.D. dissertation (The Pennsylvania State University, 1962).

³Ronald J. Matlon, "Model Speeches in the Basic Speech Course," *The Speech Teacher*, XVII (January, 1968), p. 50.

⁴Matlon, P. 51.

⁵A. Craig Baird, "Speech Models and Liberal Education," *The Speech Teacher*, XVI (January, 1967), p. 15.

⁶Matlon, p. 51.

⁷James G. Ridgeway, "The Teaching of Speech in High School Through Example," *Quarterly Journal of Speech*, XXVIII (February, 1941), p. 74.

⁸John F. Wilson and Carroll C. Arnold, *Public Speaking as a Liberal Art* (Boston, 1964), p. 327.

⁹Robert Cathcart, *Post Communication Criticism and Evaluation* (Indianapolis, 1966), p. 34.

¹⁰Matlon, p. 56.

¹¹Randall Harrison, "Nonverbal Communication: Explorations into Time, Space, Action, and Object," *Dimensions in Communication*, Edited by J. H. Campbell and H. W. Helper. (Belmont, Calif., 1965), p. 167.

II

SCIENCE AND FOREIGN LANGUAGE

Secondary curriculum specialists continue to stress the importance of the roles that both the study of science and foreign language play in the intellectual growth of youngsters. Through science young people develop an awareness of the problems that confront society and see the possibilities for working toward solutions. With the study of a foreign language students gain the ability to communicate with other cultures and are able to discover the roots of their own language. The use of audiovisuals in both fields has over the past 10-20 years become an accepted and expected practice by most secondary science and language educators.

Four articles in this section speak to the ways nonprint has been used to support the needs of the curriculum. Bert Kempers in "The Use of 8-mm Films in Teaching Biology" gives the reasons he finds the super 8mm format in science instruction more advantageous than the 16mm format. He also explains the ways he thinks films might be used in presenting biological phenomena. The reasons for using 35mm slides to teach physics are given by Francis S. Lestingi in "Projection Pointers: Copy It." Type of film to use for best results and ordering information for additional details are included. Buford L. Williams explains in "Projecting Polaroid Photographs" how and why he encourages his students to make transparencies in addition to their regular prints for laboratory experiments. Svein Oksenholt provides the reader with valuable information on how to go about placing a short-wave radio in a foreign language classroom. Advantages, techniques, and testing are examined along with an extensive annotated bibliography of sources and terminology used in radio transmission.

THE USE OF 8-mm FILMS
IN TEACHING BIOLOGY

Bert Kempers

How many of us ever give thought to why films are used in schools and, in particular, why they are used in a biology classroom? Certainly, visual materials add enriching experiences for students. Beyond that, films can do certain things that other media cannot do. They can transport students to the far corners of the world, as well as show the smallest organisms. Through the use of high-speed photography they can take an event that occurs in a fraction of a second and spread it out over a much longer period of time, or through time-lapse photography they can take an event which takes days or even months to occur and condense it into a period of a few seconds. By ordering the scenes in a film, events that are interrelated and occur at different times can be placed in juxtaposition, so that a total phenomenon takes on meaning.

Advantages of Super 8

It goes without saying that in the past 30 years there has been an expanded use of films in the classroom. By and large these have been 16-mm sound films with narrative tracks describing the events pictured on the screen. In the last six or seven years we have seen the use of other film formats. In particular, the development of continuous 8-mm cartridged loop films has been phenomenal. Today, there is hardly a subject that is not covered by these short segments of 8-mm film. The advent of Super 8 mm (trade name), as opposed to standard 8 mm, has contributed in part to the growth and utilization of 8-mm systems.

In some cases the change-over from standard 8 to Super 8 has caused hardships. School systems equipped with standard-8 projectors have had to consider changing over to the improved Super-8 format. The change is worth the effort, for not only are the pictures several times brighter in the Super 8 format, but projection equipment is more reliable and provides a steadier picture. Largely this is because standard 8 was simply a stepchild of 16-mm films, whereas the Super-8 film was designed for small-format projection. This design included the larger image area as well as redesigned sprocket holes, placed so that the total projection is improved. The steadier image in Super 8 is accounted for by the smaller sprocket holes, which are placed in the center of the frame rather than on the frame line. This gives a more positive registration in the projector and results in a flowing sequence of pictures that do not jump around on the screen. Of more recent date is the advent of sound films in the 8-mm format. Unfortunately, there are no standards in the 8-mm field at this time, and different projectors require different kinds of sound systems as well as cartridges or reels: 8-mm sound films

Reprinted by permission of the author and *American Biology Teacher* 32 (March 1970):170-72.

and 8-mm silent films are not interchangeable, even among systems developed by the same manufacturer.

In a very short time the quality of 8-mm printing has been vastly improved, so that today it is difficult to tell whether the print being projected is a 16-mm or a Super-8-mm print. Most of the 8-mm projectors with sound systems are considerably quieter than the 16-mm projectors typically found in classrooms. Of importance to school systems is the fact that projectors and films are considerably cheaper in the smaller format. This means simply that a film library can maintain more titles for the same amount of money.

The Ideal in Biology Films

What should be the characteristics of an ideal film for teaching biology? This was a question asked of many teachers and educators when BSCS initiated its film program. There is, of course, no simple answer; but the following is a list of characteristics identified as having definite advantages:

1. Films should be four or five minutes long (although by selective stops the presentation of these films might take much longer). Most biologic phenomena can be depicted in a film of this length; at the same time a film of this length costs considerably less than a longer film.

2. Films should limit the subject matter to a single phenomenon or a few related phenomena. This is so that the teacher wishing to teach one idea or to depict one phenomenon does not have to take up valuable classroom time by using a film that considers a variety of problems, of which only one or two are important to the class.

3. The film should involve subject matter or techniques that cannot be handled in the normal high-school laboratory. This might include experiments that are too difficult to undertake and procedures that are too long to develop; or the films may have to do with concepts that involve movement either in time or space.

4. Narrative sound-tracks should be limited or eliminated. Natural synchronous sound can be beneficial if the sounds are important to the understanding of a concept — for example, where audible signals are related to a behavioral phenomenon.

5. Films and projectors should be easily accessible.

Advantages of Film Loops

Many teachers would use more films if they had them in their classroom at the time when they were needed. Most teachers do not like scheduling motion pictures and equipment months in advance, primarily because it is difficult to correlate the arrival of a film with the course content. In order to make more films and projectors available, materials must be inexpensive so that teachers can have easy access to them.

How do loop cartridges fit these criteria? To begin with, the films are short—never over four minutes long—but they can be stopped to provide a longer presentation. Because of the length of the films, phenomena that can be depicted are naturally limited to a single loop. The teacher can decide when a film will do a better job or when the subject can be handled better in the laboratory. The loop cartridges do not have sound tracks. As suggested above, films and projectors should be easily accessible. Five or six loop-cartridge projectors can be purchased for the price of one 16-mm projector, and approximately 20 loops can be purchased for the price of a single 30-minutes 16-mm production.

There are several different kinds of Super-8-mm loop-cartridge projection systems, and not all films are available in all systems. In addition to the loop cartridges, reel-to-reel Super 8-mm is still very much in use by home movie photographers and is gaining in use by teachers. Provided the films are silent Super 8-mm, they can usually be recartridged for any silent Super-8-mm system. Projector manufacturers can supply names of film laboratories where the films can be recartridged for a particular kind of projector. Films cartridged for one sound system will not work with another sound system.

Is 16-mm Obsolete?

At this time it is too early to tell which systems will persist and which will be best for classroom use. Super 8-mm for classroom use is so new that all projector manufacturing companies are still improving their systems.

What we have suggested so far may be interpreted to mean that 16-mm sound films as we have grown to know them may be on their way out. I personally do not feel that this is true. There are places for the longer sound films, although I think for most showings Super-8-mm sound equipment is perfectly adequate. I think, rather, that we are adding a dimension to our visual aids when we use loop cartridges. I do not think that loops will replace the longer sound films, nor do I think they should. It is almost like the trite comparison of apples with oranges. Sound films and short 8-mm films are simply two different things, and I do not believe that they should present the teacher with an either-or-decision. There are many good sound films around, and they should be used where they can add to the total classroom situation.

Film as a Laboratory Tool

In the past few years, I have often been asked whether I thought a film could replace a laboratory experience. I see no reason why a film should replace a laboratory experience; rather, it is quite possible that a film can become a part of the laboratory. The motion-picture camera is a perfectly good scientific tool. In the area of behavior there are few better. Professional scientists studying the behavior of organisms often use motion-picture film for a variety of purposes—for example, to record types of behavior that occur only during a very limited portion of a year. Then, too, it is much easier to take measurements from a film than it is to take these measurements from nature. Students can observe films and analyze them much as a professional scientist would.

Film expands the laboratory so that it encompasses the whole world. New films for the biological sciences are being designed to involve the audience. Early examples are the botany films developed by the Iowa State University Film Group and the BSCS Single Topic films. The latter are designed to involve students in an experience in science; that is, the students must pose questions, raise problems, interpret experimental data, and challenge each other. Rather than being purely descriptive, these films require student and teacher participation. Other producers are developing similar films at this time. In many of the new films questions are asked: these are designed to encourage classroom discovery and individual inquiry. The success of these films and the experiences they provide depend in large part on the preparation that the teacher puts into the presentation. The teacher must study the film, ahead of time, along with the accompanying guides and note material.

Basically, there are three ways in which a teacher may wish to use 8-mm films in presenting biological phenomena. One is the descriptive manner in which we have viewed films for many years. Another is the inquiry format: the class is asked to interact with material presented on the screen. Yet another way permits the individual student or small groups of students to use film to study specific behaviors. In a laboratory experience, the teacher may wish to supply more than one film for student consideration. In this case, the teacher may pose questions for the students to investigate; or the students may form their own questions and try to learn something about the question which they have posed, by using film as data.

PROJECTION POINTERS:
COPY IT

Francis S. Lestingi

The available literature in technical physics, the history of physics, and popularized physics offers a wealth of visual material that can be utilized in an effective manner in most physics courses. Yet despite this availability there remains the difficulty of transforming the material into a visible and convenient form for use in the classroom. Perhaps the least effective means for displaying visual material from a printed source is the *opaque projector*. The bulkiness of this projector alone makes its use less than satisfactory. The optics provide only a moderately bright projected image even in a relatively dark room. Moreover, operation of the opaque projector must be from the rear of the room and extreme caution must be exercised to insure that the printed copy does not overheat from the intense output of the light source.

It is equally impractical to attempt to produce an overhead projection transparency of the desired printed visual material. One would first have to produce a xerographic copy of the original and then a standard thermographic transparency. Any color in the original would of course be lost in this technique; and if the original were not substantial in size, the projected image would be inadequate for proper viewing.

One of the best media for displaying material from printed sources seems to be the 35mm color transparency slide. This medium permits one to crop, enlarge, and "edit" the printed material as it is being photographed. Additionally, colors in the original can be maintained faithfully. Producing 35mm slides offers little difficulty if the proper equipment is available. One needs a good single-lens reflex 35mm camera, close-up tubes or close-up lenses, proper film and lighting, and a copy stand.

Several types of film can be utilized depending on the lighting conditions. If available light is to be used, in a library for example, one may use a fast film with an ASA 500 (manufactured by GAF). Under artificial lighting conditions one may use a variety of ASA ratings. Some manufacturers now offer an interesting color transparency film labeled "5254." With electronic flash this film has an ASA 100. It may also be force processed up to ASA 200 or ASA 400. In addition the processor returns a set of mounted color slides *plus* color negatives from which color prints can be made. Thus slides can be made for class use and prints can be produced for offices, corridors, classroom, labs, etc. (One source of "5254" film is RGB Color Laboratories, 849 North Highland Avenue, Hollywood, CA 90038).

A copy stand is essential for producing crisp, close-up photographs. With the aid of close-up tubes or lenses one can produce excellent quality slides of

Reprinted by permission of the author and *Physics Teacher* 13 (April 1975):243. Copyright © 1975 by The American Association of Physics Teachers.

original material as small as a postage stamp and as large as a magazine page. Details for the construction of the stand may be found in Kodak's Audiovisual Data Book S-8, *Producing Slides and Filmstrips*. (Available from Eastman Kodak Company, Motion Picture and Education Markets Division, Eastman Kodak Company, Rochester, NY 14650, $1.75).

PROJECTING POLAROID PHOTOGRAPHS   Buford L. Williams

Two problems that arise when the class uses Polaroid photography in the Project Physics laboratory experiments are: (1) A good deal of film is used in trying to produce enough copies of usable quality prints for each group of students. (2) There is not enough time for the teacher to help each group analyze the information from its photos. One can minimize these problems by preparing a transparency for the overhead projector (from a black-and-white Polaroid photograph) and using it to explain the phenomena under investigation.

The transparency is made from the emulsion, which is separated from the paper backing of the photo after it has been exposed to acetone vapor. To prepare the transparency you will need:

Acetone
4-inch transparent book tape or transparent Contact® Paper
Scissors
Wide-blade putty knife
3-pound coffee can with a tight-fitting plastic lid
Two 50 ml beakers

After the photo has been taken, do not apply the usual Polaroid coating material. Pour 5 ml of acetone into the bottom of the coffee can and support the print on two 50 ml beakers so that the print does not touch the liquid acetone. Close the can with the plastic lid, and leave the picture in the acetone vapor for 10 minutes. The vapor loosens the emulsion so that it can be peeled from the paper. While the photo is in the can, prepare a 5¾ x 4-inch piece of the transparent paper or book tape. At the end of the 10 minutes, lay the print face up on a smooth surface. Using the putty knife, press the transparent material over the photograph, being careful to avoid air bubbles. Press down firmly and then peel the transparent material and the emulsion from the white backing paper with a steady pull. The emulsion can be laminated between two sheets of transparent material if it is to be saved for future use.

The transparency should be used as a supplement to the students' laboratory work. Students will enjoy making transparencies from their photos and will be motivated to better efforts when they can show the results of their work to the other students via this medium. Often students will get exceptionally revealing photos from which the entire class can profit. Several usable transparencies can be kept on hand for those occasions when everything goes wrong in the lab, or the film supply is depleted before sufficient photos are obtained.

Reprinted by permission of the author and *Science Teacher* 41 (March 1974):41.

Reference

"Polaroid Photography." *Teachers Resource Book — The Project Physics Course.* Holt, Rinehart and Winston, Inc., New York, Toronto. 1970. Pp. 91-96.

PUT A SHORT-WAVE RADIO IN YOUR
FOREIGN LANGUAGE CLASSROOM

Svein Oksenholt

The foreign language teacher who wants to bring live foreign language broadcasts directly into the classroom will find it useful to try shortwave listening (SWL).[1] Only some elementary knowledge of shortwave radio receivers and antenna construction is really necessary. Although there are over 3,000 shortwave stations in the world, we—the foreign language teachers—are interested in only about a dozen of them. This is for a variety of reasons, primarily relating to the wattage of the transmitter or perhaps the time of the day.

Of the 14 international and domestic shortwave bands, only two or three will be of use at a particular time of the year. Don't become awed by the magnitude of SWL options, because only a few of these programs are of sufficient quality for your students' use. Any local radio electronics firm should be happy to discuss with you the concepts of selectivity, sensitivity, and stability. If you plan to buy a shortwave radio for classroom use, members of an amateur high school or college club should be able to explain the audio significance of these terms.

Wavelength

The numbers in Figure 1 should be learned by any teacher who wants to use the shortwave radio for program dubbing purposes. Daytime listening or dubbing should be limited to the higher frequencies. Dubbing can be done in the evening hours if you are listening on the 49, 41, 31, or 25 meter bands. Before dubbing any commercial programs of dramatic or literary content, be sure to check with the broadcasting station to avoid possible copyright violation.

Figure 1

Meter Bands	75,	49,	41,	31,	25,	19,	16,	13,	11
Megahertz (frequency)	3.9	6	7	9	11	15	17	21	25

Antenna

One factor in achieving good reception of a shortwave program is the density and height of the ionosphere, which reflects radio waves back to the earth. Another important factor is the use of a professionally designed shortwave antenna. The antenna lead-in wires must also be appropriately shielded. I have

Reprinted by permission of the author and the Association for Educational Communications and Technology from *Audiovisual Instruction* 22 (May 1977):19-22.

successfully used the Mosely SWL-7 trap antenna kit in several schools for reception on the 11, 13, 16, 19, 25, 31, 41, and 49 meter bands. Any seasoned high school radio amateur could put this antenna kit together in less than an hour—and the price of the kit is quite reasonable.

Advantages

Shortwave listening offers many advantages to the foreign language class.[2] (1) It provides practical information. (2) It is alive. (3) It is entertaining. (4) It represents an addition to the foreign language. (5) It has superior interest value. (6) Current events broadcasts contribute to the learning of a meaningful vocabulary. (7) It is the language used and heard by the natives. (8) The Gestalt image is kept intact. (9) Cultural tidbits are offered daily. (10) It provides a variety of intonations, expressions, linguistic phenomena, voices, subject matter, affective domain learning areas, novelties, achievement experiences, and curricular innovations.

Techniques

The initial steps involved in putting together a meaningful unit of an individualized subject matter package include the following.[3] (1) Write a script of the broadcast you have taped. (2) Write out questions based on these recordings. (3) Write out the performance objectives of each learning unit of recorded material that has been supplied with a script. Make the description as simple as possible—although all four parts (purpose of the behavior, description of the behavior, the conditions under which they are to occur, and the criteria by which they are to be evaluated) should, if possible, be given. (4) Let the students read the script out loud. (5) Extract key (audio) sentences or phrases from the broadcast, let the students repeat them after the announcer, let them compare the differences in intonation, stress, pitch, etc. Use the pause button if needed to temporarily stop the tape. (6) Ask for synonyms or antonyms of the vocabulary found in the script. (7) Write brief dialogs using the script as source material. (8) Ask questions based on these dialogs. (9) Provide for a question-and-answer blackboard contest—boy-girl, left row-right row, etc.—to ascertain the champions of the day. Use the script and the recorded radio broadcast for reference.

Testing

In spite of the fact that foreign language testing—or any other form of educational measurements for that matter—is not yet an exact science, we nevertheless have certain intrinsic opinions as to what good testing in a foreign language is all about.[4] (1) We want as many target language test items included as possible, and we do not want to rely too much on English-to-target-language exercises. (2) We would all like to use more graphic representations, pictures, dramatizations, paraphrasing in the target language, synonyms, antonyms, cognates, idioms, flashcards, journal cutouts, games, crossword puzzles, menus, and many other testing options. (3) Testing should deal more with principles of semantic knowledges and skills, and less with specific points of grammar enunciated in English. For example:

A. Write a + sign if the list of words have the same meaning and a ÷ sign if they are antonyms:
    1. _____ morning, evening
    2. _____ physician, doctor

B. Underline the words that are associated in thoughts:
    1. dentist, river, heart, letter, pain
    2. piano, wine, play, week, horse

C. Underline the words that are antonyms:
    1. small, fat, tall, skinny, old
    2. answer, eat, die, ask, teach

D. Underline the words that are synonyms:
    1. pretty, to be sure, red, attractive, blue
    2. laugh, smile, get up, ski, run

E. Underline the words that would complete the sentence properly:
    1. Six times six is (thirty-six) (sixty-three).
    2. There are (seven) (seventeen) days in a week.

F. Which word is related in thought to the group of words at the left? Underline it.
    1. dress
        coat ⎤— cooking, dancing, clothing
        shoes ⎦
    2. snow
        rain ⎤— mountain, weather, wood
        hail ⎦

Basic SWL Frequencies

13 Meter Band . . 21,450 to 21,750kHz
16 Meter Band . . 17,700 to 17,900kHz
19 Meter Band . . 15,100 to 15,450kHz
25 Meter Band . . 11,700 to 11,975kHz
31 Meter Band . . 9,500 to 9,775kHz
41 Meter Band . . 7,100 to 7,300kHz
49 Meter Band . . 5,950 to 6,200kHz
60 Meter Band . . 4,750 to 5,060kHz
90 Meter Band . . 3,200 to 3,400kHz

Terminology Used in Radio Transmission

English	French	German	Spanish
Frequency	Frequence	Frequenz	Frecuencia
Frequency band	Bande de frequence	Frequenzband	Banda de frecuencia
Kilocycle	Kilocycle	Kilohertz	Kilociclo
Listener	Auditeur	Hörer	Radio oyente
Program	Programme	Programm	Programa
Radio station	Radiodiffusion	Rundfunk	Radiodifusora
Shortwave	Onde courte	Kurzwelle	Onda corta
This (here) is	Iei	Hier ist	Aquí
Transmitter	Emetteur	Kurtzwellensender	Transmisora
Wave length	Longueur d'onde	Wellenlänge	Longitud de onda

Selective Annotated Bibliography

Burnell, Jerrold B., "How Shortwave Radios Can Improve Teaching Effectiveness," *Educational Technology* (October 1971), pp. 60-61.

The shortwave radio is a useful tool that is not being taken advantage of in many school systems. The radio cost is under $400, thus making it feasible to buy for most schools. Journalism, music, history, and many other subjects might devote time to the use of the shortwave programs.

The value of the shortwave radio in the study of foreign languages is unmeasurable. Programs originating in foreign countries can familiarize students with phrases they might never find in a textbook. Hearing the news and political opinions of another country can bring a student much closer to the language being studied. Since many of the clearer programs come through in the evenings, programs may be taped for later use in the classroom.

By contacting foreign language radio stations, teachers can get copies of the schedule for the month mailed to them ahead of time. Some of the AM stations in the larger cities of the United States may also be heard broadcasting foreign language programs. These programs are aimed at particular ethnic groups in the community.

Kirman, Joseph M., "Listen in on the World with a Shortwave Radio," *Teacher* (April 1973), pp. 69-72.

(1) Subtract the appropriate number of hours from Greenwich Mean Time (GMT) for your area. (2) Write to the embassies of the countries or local consulates for times and frequencies of the shortwave broadcasts that you may hear in your locality. (3) SWL automatically maintains current content information. (4) SWL requires little or no care.

Lally, Dale V., "Short Wave Receivers and the Foreign Language Teacher," *NALLD* (October 1971), pp. 37-42.

(1) Due attention must be given to the selection of the radio, log data, and possible class use of SWL. (2) The receiver should have AGC, RF, and AF controls. (3) Visit a surplus store for radio bargains. (4) See recent issues of popular electronic journals for listing of times and frequencies when programs are on the air. (5) Write, if necessary, to the embassies in Washington, DC. (6) At Marquette University, the Hammarlund HQ100 radio is being used. (7) Voice of

America (VOA) broadcasts in German daily at 7:45 a.m. on 15MHz. (8) Radio Canada transmits German at 11:45 a.m. on almost the same frequency. (9) French may be heard throughout the day on Radio Canada. (10) Spanish is transmitted daily by VOA, Radio Mexico International, and Radio Havana on the 16MHz frequency. (11) Radio Mexico is on 9.705, 11.770, and 21.704MHz frequencies.

Mohr, William, and Dale Lally, "Teaching German via Shortwave Broadcasts," *Modern Language Journal*, Vol. 57 (1973), pp. 119-124.

(1) Reports on a summer school experiment in 1971 that included an SWL unit. (2) Unit goals were to enliven the curriculum, to bring contemporary speech and topical materials into the classroom, to integrate contemporary speech into grammar instruction, to train students to listen more attentively to spoken German in longer breath groups and various intonation patterns, to provide motivation to continue with German language study, and to instill a genuine feeling of confidence in the students in the comprehension and oral production of the language. (3) Sources used were Radio Canada, Voice of America, and the professor's taped recordings made when he visited Germany. (4) Radio Canada transmitted at 11:45 a.m. on 11.325, 17.820, and 21.595MHz with 10-minute newscasts. (5) Voice of America transmitted at 7:45 a.m. on 15.325MHz daily. (6) The topic of the first day was basketball and hockey (by chance!). (7) Grammatical topics extracted included indirect discourse, passive voice, and word order in dependent clauses. (8) Oral and written tests, quizzes, and dictations were used. (9) There was an enormous expansion of vocabulary, including such words as Verseuchung, Lohnforderungen, Schlüpfwinkel, and Mondlandefähre. (10) In testing, the primary emphasis was oral, with question-and-answer, multiple choice, and dictation items. (11) It was recommended that all test questions be recorded so that the student may practice the answers ahead of time. (12) All students showed enthusiasm for the program. (13) It was recommended that the units be made short, with a maximum of 10 to 15 minutes per class hour.

Therien, Melvin G., "Learning French via Short Wave Radio and Periodicals," *French Review*, Vol. 46 (1973), pp. 1178-1183.

This article describes a program at Highland High School in St. Paul, MN, which received a $500 grant. The study of news in depth (analysis of French foreign policies, etc.) was rejected by the students. Other activities undertaken are listed here. (1) Write to the radio stations of the countries transmitting in French. (2) Sweep the frequency bands throughout the school day. The first day, 75 stations were logged in. (3) Concentrate on news, weather, sports results, etc., and don't tackle cultural programs of literary analysis. (4) Tape what you hear. (5) Watch out for impedance mismatch. (6) Duplicate enough tapes or cassettes so that each student has one. (7) Copy the script from the master tape—a very time-consuming job. Ask local residents who are native French to help you. (8) Duplicate the tape script. (9) Make a list of vocabulary and idioms recurring each day. (10) Use five minutes of tape for 50 minutes of class time initially. (11) After the recurring idioms are learned, a five-minute tape can be covered in a 30-minute class period. (12) The extra work for the teacher includes tape duplication, writing the script, duplicating, checking errors, testing and correcting, and planning new methods of using teaching material. (13) A round-table discussion should be used to conclude each unit.

Wood, Richard E., "Shortwave Radio as a Teaching Aid for German," *Unterrichtspraxis*, No. 1 (1972), pp. 36-41.

(1) Live shortwave radio in the target language provides a teaching aid of unsurpassed authenticity and directness, and remarkable student appeal. (2) It is important to differentiate between shortwave radio and amateur radio. (3) West Germany, East Germany, Austria, and Switzerland offer broadcasts in both German and English. (4) A radio should cover the 13, 16, 19, 25, 31, and 49 meter bands. (5) Evening broadcasts can be heard on the 25, 31, and 49 meter bands. (6) Deutsche Welle, from Cologne, transmits every evening from 5:00 p.m. to 11:10 p.m. (7) Use the 49 meter band during the winter months. (8) Österreichischer Rundfunk, from Vienna, transmits on 6,155kHz from 4:00 p.m. to 9:00 p.m. (9) Deusche Welle transmits on the 31 meter band on 9,565kHz at 5:00 p.m., on 9,605kHz at 7:00 p.m., and on 9,735kHz at 9:00 p.m. (10) In the summer months, use the 25 meter band on 11,795kHz. (11) Deusche Welle, from the Kigali relay station in Rwanda, Central Africa, is on the 16, 19, and 25 meter bands during the day. (12) Write to Deusche Welle, D-5 Köln I, Postfach 100 444, to have your name put on their mailing list for program schedules. (13) Sackville, New Brunswick, relays from 7:00 p.m. to 9:10 p.m. on 11,865kHz on the 25 meter band year round, and on 15,665kHz on the 19 meter band during the summer months. (14) Austria broadcasts on 9,770kHz on the 31 meter band. (15) Switzerland broadcasts on 9,535kHz on the 31 meter band. (16) Radio Berlin International, from East Germany, transmits on 5,955kHz and 9,730kHz. (17) Deusche Welle has "kurznachrichten" at 6:00 p.m., 8:00 p.m., and 10:00 p.m. (18) Beginning German students can listen to "Lernt Deutsch bei der deutschen Welle" at 6:30 p.m. and 9:30 p.m. on the 31 and 49 meter bands. (19) Radio Canada International, from Montreal, transmits from 10:45 a.m. to 11:15 a.m. on the 13, 16, and 19 meter bands, on 21,595kHz, 17,820kHz, and 15,325kHz. (20) BBC, London, transmits throughout the day. (21) HCJB, "Die Stimme der Anden," from Quito, Ecuador N.B. comes in loud and clear every night. (22) Radio Moscow. (23) Radio Japan broadcasts at 10:00 a.m. on 17,825kHz and 21,535kHz daily. (24) Radio Peking. (25) Radio Cairo. (26) Before you buy a radio, please consult with a person who knows something about SWL. (27) For proper antenna construction, write to Deusche Welle or the BBC for a brochure. (28) Record only those broadcasts that come in loud and clear. (29) The professional radio announcer speaking his native tongue is the ideal target language model for the students at any level.

Notes

[1]Diesick, Renee S., *Individualizing Language Instruction: Strategies and Methods*, 1975.

[2]Reichmann, E., ed., "Short-Wave Radio in Language Teaching," in *The Teaching of German*, 1970, pp. 304-306; Rivers, *The Psychologist and the Foreign Language Teacher*, 1964.

[3]Diesick and Valette, *Modern Language Classroom Techniques: A Handbook*, 1972.

[4]Valette, *Modern Language Testing: A Handbook*, 1972; *German Quarterly*, January 1952, pp. 27-32.

III

SOCIAL STUDIES AND HISTORY

The study of social studies and history, as envisioned by the twenty-first century curriculum specialist, should encompass the whole sweep of human experience. The modern social studies curriculum enables the young adult to conceptualize the future by understanding the reasons why events in the past have occurred using the ideas from economics, anthropology, political science, geography, and sociology for decisionmaking. Historical events have been recorded in both audio and video formats for students to examine and learn from.

In the lead article to this section, Mack J. Ryan begins by explaining the importance of having visuals to reinforce and expand a lecture. He also discusses community sources for the teacher to use in developing a slide collection and ways to use this newly-accumulated medium in the social studies classroom. Michael L. Berger in "The Application of Still Photography to the Teaching of History" provides the reader with a brief overview of the reasons for what he terms "photographic history," and then proceeds to show how students would go about developing a research project using this technique and the advantages to be reaped by both extroverted and introverted youngsters. The concluding article in this section by Paul F. Griffin is a detailed account of the benefits to be realized from the general use of photography in any classroom learning experience and, even more specifically, in the study of geography. The author develops criteria for judging the suitability of one photograph over another, discusses their value and disadvantages, explores methods for collecting and presenting photos, and concludes with a listing of other factors to be considered before using this medium.

SLIDES IN THE
SOCIAL STUDIES CLASSROOM

Mack J. Ryan

How often as a social studies teacher have you exclaimed to your students, "You should have seen ... !" Unfortunately, when you made that statement, you could only describe verbally what you had seen. And words alone can't always provide enough information to help someone visualize, and thus better understand what took place.

Why not make use of the trusty miniature camera to overcome this communication problem? Then when you say, "You should have seen ... !" you have a picture ready to tie to your description.

Because of the operational simplicity and portability of the equipment, slide programs lend themselves to a variety of instructional settings. They can be used for individualized study or repeated presentations with large and small groups of students.

Community Sources for Slide Collections

Sources of visuals for use in the social studies classroom are plentiful. Your own community is a good starting point for acquiring a varied slide collection. Post offices, museums, art galleries, cemeteries, public buildings, and centers of business and industry will yield an abundance of photographs that are appropriate for the study of local history, government, and business, as well as other areas of social studies. Post offices and public buildings often have murals that depict the historical development of the community. Examination of photographs of the workers in these facilities can help students better understand the types of services provided by government at the local, state and national levels.

Older cemeteries in the community are worth exploring with the camera. Frequently their tombstones supply valuable historical data. Art galleries and museums contain paintings, artifacts, models, and other realia that can be photographed for use in the classroom. Units on career education and economics can be beefed up with visuals obtained by visits to local businesses and industries.

The local public library and the school library are treasure chests of pictorial data. Between the covers of their books and magazines are photographs, paintings, sketches, maps, cartoons, graphs and charts. By tactfully approaching a local travel agent, you can reap a rich harvest of photographs and maps of

Reprinted by permission of the author and the Association for Educational Communications and Technology from *Audiovisual Instruction* 23 (October 1978):32-33.

foreign lands. In your home, you can photograph images of important events on television, copy pictures from magazines, newspapers, or even postcards.*

Of course, this doesn't preclude you from moving about the community and elsewhere and playing the role of photojournalist or field anthropologist. Photographs of urban blight, traffic congestion, pollution, inadequate housing and recreation facilities can drive these problems more forcefully home to your students — if they see them. Your travels to places beyond the community — to other cities, states or abroad — also permit you to photograph scenes that often are not available through commercially prepared materials.

In the Social Studies Classroom

There are many ways to use your newly-accumulated slide collection in the social studies classroom. For example, help students develop skills in values clarifications by showing photographs of workers carrying signs and picketing, or copies of propaganda posters and advertisements from newspapers and magazines. These matrials can be used to stimulate a values discussion on such topics as labor, war, and the "affluent" society.

Inquiry teaching can be enhanced with the use of visuals. For example, students can analyze photographs of the art work found in the caves of Lascaux. They can make inferences about the culture of the ancient people who once inhabited these caves of Southern France and then go to other sources to test their hypotheses.

Slides of a Roman aqueduct, the architectural features of a medieval church, a diagram of the system of checks and balances in our political system, and a topographical map can be used to increase vocabulary as well as improve understanding of social studies.

The wonders of ancient civilizations, although remote to students, can be made real and near through vivid, colorful slides. Close-up shots of jewelry and pottery, as well as views of architectural styles, can bring an ancient civilization closer to students.

Don't overlook the possibilities of using slides in the evaluation process. Develop test exercises that use slides of pictures, paintings, cartoons, graphs, and maps. Questions can be asked that require students to identify, interpret and analyze the slides they view.

Through slides, students can be helped in developing skills in critical thinking and values clarification. The past can be made more real to them, and their often distorted views of other societies can be corrected. Their social studies vocabularies can be enlarged, and their knowledge and understanding can be evaluated. Above all, they can be stimulated with slides to pursue their studies with greater vigor and interest.

---

*When copying copyrighted material, be sure you are familiar with the "Fair Use" guidelines of the new Copyright Law.

THE APPLICATION OF STILL
PHOTOGRAPHY TO THE TEACHING
OF HISTORY

Michael L. Berger

In 1967, there appeared two thin volumes devoted to an exploration of new developments in anthropological research methods. *Visual Anthropology*, by John Collier Jr.,[1] concerned itself primarily with adopting still photography for use as a research tool to clarify observed group intra-relationships. Thomas R. Williams' *Field Methods in the Study of Culture*,[2] while much broader in scope than the Collier work, also discussed the applicability of photography to the field of anthropology. Although these books had, and continue to have, an impact on scholars in that specialized field, little has been done to show their appropriateness to other areas of the social sciences. The purpose of this article is to explore the possible application of the ideas of Collier and Williams as motivational tools in the teaching of history in the elementary and secondary school classroom.

While it is true, as Collier points out, that you can not photograph the past, it is possible to photograph contemporary "artifacts" which may yield, upon analysis, historical information. Collier maintains that photographic evidence, like all data, must be abstracted. Thus, from the photographic record it should be possible to abstract those items that have historical significance.

In fact, one of the chief advantages of employing photographic research techniques is that they provide for the widest possible coverage. The photograph never forgets, while the combination of the human eye and memory may. Although Collier warns that the camera is selective in what it records, it need not be more selective than the human eye. Every place that can be examined by the naked eye can be photographed using a simple "instamatic" camera. Thus, coverage can, if the researcher so wishes, be complete.

Furthermore, what one observes with the naked eye is remembered only if it has meaning. There is the tendency for the mind to reject that which it does not understand. At the very best, that which is not understood is recorded as an "anti-fact," and little attempt is made to synthesize it with those facts which already seem to coincide with one another. With photographs, as Collier notes, it is possible to record what one does not understand, without the psychological problem of dealing with an "anti-fact." This may enable the observer to see a relationship at a later date, which would have been impossible through instantaneous naked eye observation only. It should also, as Williams claims, keep to a minimum the amount of observational distortion due to one's cultural background. Although this can not be totally eliminated, the photographic record allows the student to study the object at length, and to bring other research tools to bear on unsolved

Reprinted by permission of the author and *Social Studies* 63 (Feburary 1979):76-79. Copyright © 1972 by Heldref Publications.

problems while the object is still "there." Hopefully, this would cut down on cultural bias.

The camera, then, is to be used as a research tool. Collier points out that this runs counter to the prevailing notion that one takes photographs to illustrate something that has already been designated as important. Here, one takes pictures in order to later abstract knowledge and to verbalize it.

The application of the anthropological techniques of Collier and Williams to history would be new. What follows should be taken as one possible means by which "photographic history" could have meaning.

It would be necessary for the school to make a sizeable investment in equipment for this type of research to be carried out. In addition to cameras, the school would be called upon to provide film, flash units, and developing. Without the addition of flash, many photographs could not be taken inside buildings, and the student's field of research would be thus unnecessarily hampered. There is no need for the entire class to be working on this type of assignment at once, so that the school need not buy a camera for each student in the class. However, there should be enough cameras so that the inevitable repairs and losses will not stop a project already in motion. Developing costs could be minimized or entirely eliminated if the students did their own developing, or if it were done for them by the school's photography club. (There are learning possibilities here which, while not related to history *per se*, are very real nonetheless.)

Each student would select a topic of historical interest to him or her and one which coincides with the broad, class-wide field of investigation. It is assumed that he or she knows very little about the topic chosen. In fact, students should be encouraged *not* to do any reading on their subject (a directive most students will willingly follow). This is really an introductory exercise, meant to stimulate students for a later, in-depth study of the subject.

Each student should be given a single roll of eight or twelve exposure film. The number is purposely low for two reasons. First, it necessitates a certain amount of preliminary deductive thinking on the part of the student. He or she must narrow the possibilities down to those that seem most reasonable. A picture of a statue of Napoleon should tell more aobut that period of French history than one of a French pastry shop, though not necessarily. Secondly, while this may not be obvious to the student, careful analysis of eight different pictures is a very time consuming operation. Furthermore, as the number of pictures increases, the job of synthesizing the information becomes progressively more difficult. A report written from twenty or thirty-six exposures would tend to be a collection of disjointed observations.

For example, let us postulate that the instructor wishes to motivate a class for a study of the Napoleonic Era. Obvious locations for photographs would be statues in parks and exhibits in local museums. Should these fail or not be available (many museums will not allow flash pictures to be taken inside them), the ordinary phone book can be a gold mine. Listed under Napoleon or France one would find a collection of restaurants, friendship societies, publishers, clothing establishments, schools, theatres, churches, etc. While some of these may *seem* foolish to the untrained observer, they may not be upon examination. Incidentally, the urban school would seem to be better situated for this type of project than the suburban or rural school. The absolute number of potential "information centers" would tend to be largest in the inner city.

It would be hoped that the photographs themselves would be in color. This aspect can give meaning to an object which would not have been apparent from a black and white picture. For instance, the colors of a national flag usually symbolize something important in that country's past. However, it should also be made clear to the students that the object of the project is not to produce prizewinning photographs. Otherwise, in an effort to achieve some type of visual effect, the student may distort the meaning of the scene. To this end, it would be wise to purchase cameras with fixed focus and automatic light exposure guides. These items would also guarantee, as much as this is possible, that the pictures would come out. Furthermore, the cost to the school system would thereby be reduced. These "instamatic" cameras have the lowest initial cost and seldom need repair.

When the pictures are developed, they should be returned to the student without comment. He or she should be made to understand, though, that a report full of pictures with short captions underneath them is unacceptable. As Collier maintains, the successful photographic researcher is able to eliminate the photographs from his or her final verbal statement. However, it would seem harsh to completely bar illustrations from the final report. After all, they represent, in a crude sense, a work of art created by the student, and it is logical that he or she would want to display some of them. It would also serve as a check to make sure that the information presented did indeed evolve from the photographs rather than from book research.

Hopefully, in the development of the final report, the student would find the need to establish categories for his data and to write his report using these. While each picture is different, one of the objectives of this assignment would be to have the students select from the several pictures those aspects that "hang together," i.e. to synthesize materials. Students would thus experience both inductive and deductive thinking during the course of their project. They would also be developing the ability to verbalize from visual imagery.

Another objective would be to have the student discover that there is a difference between what John Collier calls "tangible content" and "intangible content." In other words, it would not be sufficient for the student to relate only those facts which were obvious from the photographs. He or she should be prepared to extrapolate from these facts into the realms of probability and possibility. Thus, the clothing depicted in a picture may give some insight into the period during which the personage lived. However, this is not to say that the student should be encouraged to engage in random guessing. As Williams notes, one of the positive results of studying a subject is the delineation of what you do *not* know. Students should be encouraged to follow Margaret Mead's dictate that:

> One must always know the exact place in the whole of the part that is unexplored, [and] the probable size of the unexplored area.... [3]

As it stands, both the extroverted and the introverted youngster has an equal chance to succeed in this type of assignment. "The photograph is not a 'message' in the usual sense. It is, instead, the raw material for an infinite number of messages which each viewer can construct for himself."[4] Since there are no right or wrong answers, the quiet or slow child should be willing to do his best. The extroverted student, however, may be induced to broaden his research, as Collier suggests, by using his photographs as *entreports* to an interview situation. People tend to be more willing to be interviewed if they feel they have been *selected* for some reason. Thus, the owner of a French restaurant, seeing that his establishment is to be incorporated into a report, may be quite willing to talk for awhile with the student. He could be asked, for example, why aspects of the interior (or exterior) of his restaurant were designed the way they were. Hopefully, the answers would help the student in the later process of photographic analysis.

Notes

[1]John Collier, Jr., *Visual Anthropology: Photography as a Research Method.* New York: Holt, Rinehart and Winston, 1967.

[2]Thomas R. Williams, *Field Methods in the Study of Culture.* New York: Holt, Rinehart and Winston, 1967.

[3]Margaret Mead, "Anthropology and an Education for the Future," in D. Mandelbaum *et. al.* (eds.), *The Teaching of Anthropology.* Washington, D.C.: American Anthropological Association, 1963, p. 604. (This is the Association's memoir number 94.)

[4]Paul Byers, "Cameras Don't Take Pictures," *The Columbia University Forum*, IX (Winter 1966), p. 31.

PHOTOGRAPHS IN THE CLASSROOM

Paul F. Griffin

The teaching of geography can be enhanced through the judicious use of audiovisual materials in the classroom. Since the child will have an opportunity of observing a very small part of the geographic material that he will study, effective devices must be employed to assist him in picturing vividly and accurately situations far away. The leading symbols used by the child in the expression of thought and the interpretation of the world are photographs, drawings, models, illustrations through graphs and diagrams, maps, globes, and language.

Photographs in General

Still photographs include all photographs without motion. Besides the flat picture, which is the most common, there are filmstrips, slides, and stereographs. The still picture supplies one of the best representations of realities and can contribute much to understandings in geography.[1] Other scientists, such as the chemist and the biologist, can work with materials in their laboratories, but unfortunately, the geographer cannot bring indoors for study the real subject of his analysis, for it is the face of the whole earth as modified by people. Nor can he take his students to see more than a small part of the earth. Although observation of the region being studied is naturally the most effective way of teaching geography, this is not always practical or possible. The nearest approach that the teacher of geography can make to bringing real landscapes to his class is to use photographs of them. Thus, the still picture is the best substitute for the actual landscape where human activity is shown in its natural setting.

Choosing Photographs

To be worthwhile in geographic education, photographs must be carefully selected for their value in developing vocabulary, geographic concepts, and understandings of geographic relationships. Pictures vary greatly in their geographic quality; all photographs do not have geographic value. The following classes of pictures are valuable in geography teaching: (a) pictures showing the natural landscape, (b) pictures showing the cultural landscape or manmade activities, and (c) pictures combining the natural and cultural activities.[2]

Reprinted by permission of *Journal of Geography* 69 (May 1970):291-98, National Council for Geographic Education.

Value of Photographs

Flat pictures are the oldest, the least expensive, and the most universally available of all materials of instruction. Used either alone or in conjunction with other curriculum materials, good pictures *can* help to make learning an interesting adventure in living. A picture, if wisely selected, (1) enables a student to take in at a glance a complex relationship economically and accurately, (2) recalls a concrete, specific situation, (3) gives, through its reproduction of the original, an appearance of reality, (4) is easily understood, and (5) arouses questions which will lead the student far beyond the immediate purpose of the photograph.

Whether or not photographs used as teaching tools actually *do* contribute to the learning process depends upon how the teacher structures the learning situation. For instance, it is possible to structure the situation so that it requires any one of these three responses: (a) recitation of facts, (b) facsimile of what was presented, (c) creative thinking — making extensive use of newly acquired facts and ideas in the process.

Disadvantage of Photographs

A photograph is supposed to be an accurate record, the unvarnished truth. Everyone knows, however, that photographs do lie, and most photographs present only one aspect of a subject. In fact, the photographic artist has ways of making a picture show what he wants by selecting the point of view of the camera, by controlling the lighting on the subject, by arranging the composition of the picture, and by manipulating the laboratory process afterward. Using these controls, a photographer can make a tall person, building, or tree appear to be small or a short person, building, or tree look tall. If a child has never seen a photograph of an elephant, it is not sufficient to show him a side view of an elephant and assume that he then knows what an elephant looks like. In other words, there are all kinds of photographs, and we cannot expect any one photograph to tell the whole story. But, by selecting the most representative photographs and adding expert teaching, photographs help enrich the experience of students.

Aerial Photographs

Pictures taken from the air can be very useful in the teaching of geography. An air photograph shows everything that is visible. It contains a mass of detailed information which can be extracted by careful study. It can indicate the relative sizes and the shapes of small objects and, when an overlapping pair of photos is studied in the stereoscope, it will reveal intricate shapes of the ground. The drainage pattern of an area and the characteristics of the terrain are apparent at a glance. Areas of bedrock are usually visible; the steepness of slopes may be estimated; and the types of vegetation may be identified.

The cardinal advantage of an aerial photograph is that, within a matter of a few hours, or even moments, a picture of the immediate area may be obtained. Various types of structures, such as buildings, roads, bridges, railroads, and fields are shown in their true proportions.

Stereoscopic Examination

One of the most valuable characteristics of aerial photographs is the fact that they may be viewed stereoscopically. When this is done, the photograph resembles a small-scale relief model of the area—houses and trees stand up above the earth's surface, and minor topographic irregularities are strikingly apparent. Features of the terrain that can never be interpreted from a contour map, even by a skilled reader, are sometimes visualized stereoscopically by the most inexpert layman.

For stereoscopic examination it is necessary that adjoining prints, made on the same flight and taken at the same altitude, overlap about 60 percent. After some practice, a person of normal vision, with both eyes of equal strength, can view two prints stereoscopically without instruments. This is done by bringing some easily recognized object on one print close to its counterpart on the other. The eyes are relaxed and focused on some distant object. Then, while the pupils are kept spaced for the distant view, the eyes are made to look at the two prints until the images fuse. When this is accomplished, the photographs appear three-dimensional.

Disadvantages of Aerial Photographs

The chief disadvantage of the aerial photograph is that it is a perspective picture. Objects on it do not appear at their true distance apart, and if the relief is considerable, they are not shown in their true directions with respect to one another. If the camera is tilted at the time the picture is taken, a further error is introduced. Since distortion is least near the center of the photograph, it is customary to allow a 60 percent overlap between prints.

A second disadvantage is the lack of any known elevations on the photograph. It is not possible to determine the gradient of slopes or the height of ridges or to construct profiles as may be done on contour maps. This same principle applies in comparing a painting with a photograph of the same landscape. In the painting certain features may be emphasized and others subordinated.

Negative Relief

To a person unfamiliar with the characteristics of aerial photographs, the relief may appear at first to be inverted; that is, the tops of hills seem to be depressions, and rivers look as if they flowed along ridge crests.

This effect is likely to disappear if the picture is oriented so that the north edge of the map (for a photograph taken in the Northern Hemisphere) is held toward the observer. If this is done, the shaded side of a ridge is nearest the observer, and the light appears to be coming toward him.

Collecting Photographs

The modern textbooks have many excellent pictures. There are numerous supplementary sources, including newspapers, magazines, postcards, and advertising materials. *The National Geographic, Life, Look, Time, Fortune*, and numerous petroleum magazines — *Standard Oil Bulletin, Aramco World, Orange Disc, Petroleum Today, The Lamp, Imperial Oil Review*, and *Ethyl News* — plus the rotogravure section of the Sunday newspapers are valuable sources. Every school should have a collection of pictures to illustrate the various topics of geography. This is particularly true of the lower grades, where the child is building up his initial geographic concepts. Students should be encouraged to make individual collections and to organize these collections under appropriate headings.

The supplementary photographs of the school may be classified and filed in envelopes with the general topic and the particular photographs indicated on the backs of the envelopes. The photographs, when needed, may be withdrawn from the files and clasped to cardboards. If it seems preferable, each photo may be mounted on a cardboard and the mounted photos may be carefully classified and filed.

Availability of Slides

The most common source of slides are commercial producers, school or teacher-pupil produced slides, and those secured from individuals. Some commercial producers of slides specialize in educational materials and sell slides individually or in sets on various subjects. Other sources may be companies which give or loan slides concerning their products, plants, or educational projects in which the companies have interests. Still another source of commercially-produced slides are the photographic stores and photographers who will photograph and make slides for individuals or schools as a regular part of their work.

A set of slides may be built up over a period of time by the school as a regular part of its program, either as a class project or as a special project. Slides may be borrowed from individuals, given to schools by individuals, or they may be borrowed from individuals and duplicate copies made for school use.

Presenting Photographs

A still picture may be presented to the class as a flat picture, as a filmstrip, as a slide, or as a transparency. Ordinarily, the last three must be seen, and this, in turn, involves a partly darkened room, a screen, and a projector. Because of this equipment and preparation the showing is to a group, with the benefits of a social situation.

Flat Pictures

Flat pictures can either be held up for the whole class to see or be examined individually by the pupils. They may be placed on a table in any order, and the students may be asked to arrange them in logical order so as to show causes and effects or successive changes in sequence. Pictures dealing with a topic under discussion may be mixed with irrelevant pictures, and students may be asked to select the pertinent pictures.

Students may be asked to make a list of appropriate questions dealing with each picture. The ability of students to interpret pictures and to use them as organizing centers may be tested (1) by presenting them with a picture and appropriate questions, (2) by distributing pictures, each with a number, the students to write opposite the same numbers on a sheet the important thing represented, (3) by giving students the names of the pictures and asking them to place beside each the appropriate number as indicated on the picture. In journey-geography work, students can "think through" the details of a trip more successfully if they have pictures illustrating the appealing scenes along the route. The student may describe the journey in relation to the pictures. The details may vary, but the teacher will attempt to use the pictures in such a way that he secures a maximum of worthwhile mental activity from each member of the class.

Filmstrips

The filmstrip is the most convenient and compact way of projecting pictures. The disadvantage of the typical filmstrip is that it has a fixed sequence. Neither can the individual pictures of the filmstrips be differently arranged nor can the pictures of local interest be added.

Slides and Transparencies

Both slides and transparencies, however, like the flat picture, can be shown in any order, and best of all, local photographs can be taken on a miniature camera and added to the material to enliven it and make it more meaningful.

From the standpoint of their teaching value, availability, simplicity, and flexibility of projection, slides are one of the most versatile of all projected materials. The economy and portability of slide projectors also enhance the use of slides in the classroom.

A unique feature of the slide is its flexibility of use. Slides may be projected in sequence, one or more may be selected for projection, or they may be used in combination with slides from other sets. A slide may be projected on the screen for an indefinite period of time without damage. This enables the teacher and the students to point out and discuss in detail items appearing on the screen. Slides may also be projected in rooms that are not totally dark, enabling the teacher to maintain visual contact with the class. This also makes it possible for the students to take notes.

The 2 x 2-inch slide is one of the more economical teaching materials. Slides may be purchased commercially in sets or individually at a cost of one dollar or less per slide. Slides may also be produced by the school either in black-and-white or in color for less than fifty cents each. It is possible to add individual slides to sets or to remove those that are no longer desired. This flexibility adds to the economy of slide use and becomes an important factor in keeping slide sets up-to-date.

The Suggestion of Photographs

A photograph is of value because of what it actually teaches and because of what it suggests. Some questions can be definitely answered from the study of a photo; some questions can be answered inferentially; while other questions may be suggested by the photo study, but other materials may be required for satisfactory answers. In the verification of inferences other sources may be consulted. If the student, for example, is looking at a photo of a truck garden, he may be able to identify certainly the sprinkling system, he may infer that the growing vegetation consists of radishes, lettuce, and onions, but he may find it necessary to consult the descriptive material to verify this inference. He may want to know the location of the gardener's market, and it may be necessary for him to consult the context and to locate the city on a map. With the photo of a part of a truck garden as a point of departure he may answer questions directly related to the photo, and widening his viewpoint he may use the photograph as an organizing center for a large body of related knowledge. It is better to make a careful study of a few photographs than to dazzle the student with a large number of photos which are flashed before him in rapid succession. Photographs should become meaningful centers for large bodies of knowledge, and exceeding care should therefore be exercised in their selection.

Great care must be taken in the selection of photographs for study in geography. In photograph selection both mechanical aspects and instructional aspects must be considered. Certain general criteria for photo selection are almost self-evident.

Mechanical Aspects

Is the photograph clear and forceful? Is the detail clear and large enough for study? Is the photograph large enough for group study or should it be used by one individual at a time? Is it pleasing and interesting? Does it have a definite center of interest? Does it direct attention to the most significant facts rather than to unimportant details?

Instructional Aspects

Is the picture authentic? Does it cover information which the student needs? Is it relevant to some essential truth which is to be taught? Does it answer questions, explain or clarify concepts? Is it related to the subject being taught? Are photographs in a series arranged in logical order? Do they show continuity of a thought or a procedure?

Other Things to Remember

The use of photographs is not self-taught. As in reading, the child needs to have his attention directed to the things he can expect to find in photographs. He needs to develop the habit of going to photographs to find ways of living and making a living in all lands; to notice features which indicate the nature of the surroundings in which those activities are carried on and features which indicate all the many other things that help him understand why people live as they do. Too long, teachers have assumed that students study photographs of their own accord; too often, teachers have also assumed that because every child can see the picture, he understands and interprets it in the right way. However, research studies reveal that the majority of children do not even glance at photographs in the text. Those who do notice illustrations often learn little from them.

Before a teacher can train a child in the use of photographs, he himself must know how to read and understand them. He must train the child first in observing photographs, actually looking at them attentively and seeing what is presented. Children need to be taught to "see" rather than merely to "look." Then, they must be led to interpret what they see and to draw conclusions. For example, by the time a child has studied regional-type geography in the fifth grade, he may draw these conclusions from a photograph showing sheep being herded in a high mountain pasture: the probable time of year, the temperature, rainfall, and climate by noting the clothing worn by the herder and by the abundance or scarcity of vegetation.

Other factors in using photographs include the following:

1. Skill in reading photographs must be developed consistently.

2. Too many photographs should not be used at once since this tends to confuse the child.

3. Photograph study should be correlated with map work.

4. Filmstrips and slides can often be more effective than sound moving films because the former can be stopped for comment and discussion.

5. The same photograph can be used at different grade levels. In the first grade, it may be used to identify a particular item, while in the intermediate grades it might be used to interpret relationships.

6. Photographs which show typical geographical features rather than those which stress the unusual should be used.

7. Size of objects, distances, and relief patterns need to be interpreted in terms of what the child knows.

8. Only questions to which answers can be found in the photographs should be used. It is bad pedagogy to ask children how many sheep they can count in a view of a closely bunched flock. The child becomes frustrated at attempting the impossible. Such a picture could be used to define the word "flock" or to show how the herder and dog move the flock from one pasture to another.

Conclusion

Conclusions from this study indicate that:

1. Photographs are considered today an important tool or device in teaching geography. They are not just to be looked at but to be read.

2. In order to gain the valuable learnings inherent in photographs, children must be taught to observe carefully and to interpret what they see.

3. Learning from pictures is not acquired incidentally, but results from carefully planned study activities.

4. Skill in reading photographs is useful in developing geographical concepts, but photographs alone are not sufficient. Geographic understandings are acquired by the combined use of photographs, textual materials, maps, globes, and observation of real landscapes.

Sources of Photographs

Aero Service Corp., Photogrammetric Engineers, 210 E. Courtland St., Philadelphia, Pa. 19120. Aerial photographs of geographical locations. Vertical prints, 9x9 inches, $10-$20; oblique prints, 7x9 inches, $1; 8x10 inches, $2.50; 11x14 inches, $3.

Airlines. Write to director of information, foreign and domestic airlines, i.e., United, Pan Am, TWA, Panagra, Varig. Indicate the type of photos desired. Most airlines will mail them free to teachers.

American Museum of Natural History, Photography Department, Central Park West at 81st St., New York, N.Y. 10024. Range of study print subjects too great for detailed listing. State specific needs, planned use. Contact prints, 4x5 inches, 5x7 inches, 8x10 inches, $2 each.

American Petroleum Institute, 1271 Avenue of the Americas, New York, N.Y. 10020. Free maps, charts, booklets, photos, and filmstrips on petroleum, junior and senior high school.

Association of American Railroads, Educational Relations, Transportation Building, Washington, D.C. 20006. 32 tinted photographic reproductions, 8½x11 inches, on 2 large sheets – 16 pictures each.

Audio-Visual Enterprises, 911 Laguna Rd., Pasadena, Calif. 91105. Study prints – wild animals of Pioneer America; 8 prints; color; habits of animals on back of prints; $15.

Bank of Hawaii, Head Office, P.O. Box 2900, Honolulu, Hawaii 96802. A large collection of photos covering many facets of the islands – economy, history, geography, travel; free.

British Information Service, 45 Rockefeller Plaza, New York, N.Y. 10020. Excellent photo source; please specify category; free.

British Travel Association, 239/243 Marylebone Roade, London, N.W.I., England. Very cooperative; large photo file on the United Kindgom and British Overseas Possessions.

California State Chamber of Commerce, 330 Bush Street, San Francisco, Calif. 94104. Lucrative source for California culture, landscapes, agriculture, transportation, manufacturing, and related topics.

Canadian Government Travel Bureau, Ottawa, Canada. A 130-page travel planning kit with 200 photos; 4 maps; free.

Cook, David C., Elgin, Ill. 60120. 9x12-inch pictures in sets of 12; color; $1.98 per set; sets are organized around community, farm, food and nutrition, plants and seeds, and transportation.

Denoyer-Geppert Co., 5235 Ravenswood Ave., Chicago, Ill. 60640. Pictures: color; typical size, 29x39 inches; topics include economic geography, animal life, habitat studies; send for picture catalog.

Encyclopaedia Britannica Educational Corp., 425 N. Michigan Ave., Chicago, Ill. 60611. Set of color prints: *Day and Night and the Seasons*; 10 prints, 13x18 inches in vinyl pouch, $9.50.

Embassies. Write to director of publicity for photos from the country or countries desired. Be definite in your request, i.e., landscapes, urban, agriculture, manufacturing, etc. Material will be supplied free to teachers.

Fideler Visual Teaching, 31 Ottawa Ave., N.W., Grand Rapids, Mich. 49502. Photos: *Life in America* (8 portfolios); *Life in Europe* (10 portfolios); *Life in Other Lands* (10 portfolios); *Social Studies* (15 portfolios); $2.95 or $3.95 depending on the number of pictures.

Freer Gallery of Art, Smithsonian Institution, Washington, D.C. 20560. Photos of objects in the gallery; 8½x10 inches; $.75 each.

Friendship Press, 475 Riverside Dr., New York, N.Y. 10027. World friends picture albums; black and white; 13x10 inches. Wide variety of topics: $1.50 per album.

General Motors Corp., Public Relations Staff, General Motors Bldg., Detroit, Mich. 48202. 14 charts (some in color) on automobiles, power, social studies; 22x34 inches; free to teachers.

Griffin, Paul F., Social Science Dept., Oregon College of Education, Monmouth, Oregon 97361. Large collection of 35mm color on most parts of the world, including agriculture, people, landscapes. Available at cost of reproduction plus packing and mailing charge to teachers or education personnel.

Hagstrom Co., 311 Broadway, New York, N.Y. 10007. Pictorial maps of the U.S., foreign countries; various sizes; most maps, $1.50 each.

Netherlands Information Service, 711 Third Ave., New York, N.Y. 10017. Set of pictures on the Netherlands. Free.

Nystrom, A. J., and Co., 3333 Elston Ave., Chicago, Ill. 60618. Geography pictures; Europe (14 pictures), Africa (16 pictures), North America (12 pictures), Australia-New Zealand-Oceania (7 pictures); color; 30x21 inches; wood frame available with each set of pictures. Prices range from $13.50 per set to $39.50 per set. Send for catalog.

Oil Industry Information Committee. Ask local dealer for address of office serving your state. Standard Oil Co. of New York, New Jersey, Ohio, and California are excellent sources. Imperial Oil, Ltd., of Canada is another valuable outlet.

Pan American Union, Photographic Library, 17th Street and Constitution Avenue, N.W., Washington, D.C. 20006. Scenes from member nations and black and white photographic prints for loan; write for information.

Silver Burdett Co., Special Products Dept., Morristown, N.J. 07960. *Families Around the World Service*; primary grades; 6 cards/12 photos; color; 19x23 inches; $14; topics: Japan, France, Kenya, Brazil, United States.

Society for Visual Education. 1345 Diversey Parkway, Chicago, Ill. 60614. Study prints; set of 8 pictures, $8; 6 or more sets, $7 per set; topics: Children of Africa, Asia, North America, South America, Australia, and Pacific Islands.

State Chambers of Commerce. Write to director of publicity for state or states. Specify types of photos desired.

United Nations, Public Inquiries Unit, Dept. of Public Documents Service, New York, N.Y. Write for information.

Notes

[1]Edith Putnam Parker, "Pictures as Laboratory Materials in Geography," *Education*, LXIV (March 1944), 434-37.

[2]National Society for the Study of Education. *The Teaching of Geography*. Thirty-Second Yearbook. (Bloomington, Ill.: Public School Printing Co., 1933), pp. 385-94.

IV

ART AND MUSIC

The enthusiasm that is generated for the fine arts during a student's elementary experience needs to be continued on the secondary level. As Trump and Miller point out in *Secondary School Curriculum Improvement*, "All students need experiences in understanding music and the various art forms. These experiences should be extensive enough to include something for those who create, those who perform, and those who consume."[1] Even with an ever increasing emphasis on the need to stress the basics, school programs should reflect a balance with a variety of course offerings available in music and art.

All four articles in this section cover unique ways to extend the student encounters with art and music. Al Hurwitz in "Turned-On Art" discusses the development of an art program on the junior high school level combining traditional art media with the newer media/technology. The blending of the two generated excitement not only from the students but from teachers in other subject areas. Richard Grillotti has written in "Anyone Can Make a Filmstrip" a convincing descriptive narrative on how his class produced an art filmstrip used as part of an assembly program with a discussion on color and abstract art without a 35mm camera. Instructions are given as well as materials needed to complete the project. Emily Scott in "The Hand-Made Slide: Whetstone for Perceptual Acuity" shows how a student's perceptual acuity might be sharpened by creating an original slide to share with classmates. In "Using Visual Media in Music," Ruth Zinar reports on the reasons for the benefits of visual aids in a music class, and then provides the reader with examples of how to go about integrating the two to enrich the students' understanding of music. Although the last article in this section by B. Lee Cooper and entitled "Popular Music: A Creative Teaching Resource" speaks to the user of popular music in the social studies classroom specifically, it is included here since its major emphasis is on the creative use of music with students. The teaching strategies to motivate student interest, which conclude the article, could be used by the English, art, or music teacher as well as the social studies instructor.

Notes

[1]J. Lloyd Trump and Delmas F. Miller, *Secondary School Curriculum Improvement: Meeting Challenges of the Times* (Boston: Allyn and Bacon, 1979), p. 98.

TURNED-ON ART

Al Hurwitz

At eight o'clock the auditorium darkens, the audience hushes for the tingling moment of curtain time. The stage appears almost bare: just the white surfaces of a huge screen flanked by two smaller screens on either side. A thunderclap cacaphony of acid rock shatters the quiet. Abstract geometric shapes start weaving crazily across the center screen, and stabs of colored light flash onto the side screens. From the wings and aisles figures close in toward the stage and start "grooving," their shadows mingling grotesquely with the screen shapes, their swaying bodies stained in whirlpools of color.

This is not the Electric Circus or some way-out discotheque. This is a group of sixth-graders reporting on the year's art program to the PTA of their Newton, Mass., school.

The presentation stresses the creative use of media, and the children demonstrate their abilities in this area in various ways: A team of three manipulates devices that control the passage of light in the overhead projector; others operate the 16mm sound projector, the two slide projectors, and the tape machine, while readers post themselves by a microphone.

This production was planned to go beyond the state of euphoria that characterizes most shows that depend on the effective use of light. The children were presenting serious information about the art program in their school during the past year, and they had given much thought to the show's content. They had obtained examples of paintings and other art work produced in class and had developed them as slides, films, and tapes in ways that composed a message. Since the materials thus presented would be preserved for future viewing by other students and teachers, one could even say that this sixth-grade class had produced curriculum as well as entertainment and information.

Three years ago I arrived at Newton to discover that media seemed to be operating everywhere except in the art program. There were reasons for this, of course. Few institutions preparing teachers of art have shifted from traditional art training to information theory, new media, and other aspects of educational technology; hence most art teachers have little in background or training to prepare them for the inroads which the intermedia movement is making on the psyches of the young. Indeed most of them lack even a basic course in the handling of audiovisual equipment. Say "media," and the average art teacher thinks art school concepts: clay, oils, pastels, paper, crayons, and the like.

Actually, the children were somewhat better prepared than their teachers for the new media consciousness in the arts program, having been conditioned since infancy by McLuhan's "environment of communications." The youngsters, however, were unaware of their readiness for such activity until it was introduced to them as a respectable component of the art program.

Reprinted by permission of the author and *American Education* 6 (March 1970):14-17.

In order for teachers to make this introduction, they themselves had to be convinced of the visual potential of the audiovisual hardware available at the school, much of it purchased under the National Defense Education Act. They also had to be educated to handle the equipment for its creative rather than its instructional values. That is, they had to put into the hands of the student the whole audiovisual paraphernalia of TV, films, slides, the camera, portable videotape and sound equipment as a natural extension of more familiar art materials. These carriers of information thus would move the teacher's concern for the components of art into wider, more contemporary spheres of time, motion, space, light, and sound.

Finally, teachers needed some grasp of the subculture of their students. Eliot Eisner of Stanford University makes the distinction between two curriculums: the explicit curriculum, which is provided by the schools; and the implicit curriculum — that value system the child brings with him to the school and is asked to discard before entering the building. Even if the implicit curriculum is not overtly denigrated by the administration, it certainly is not honored.

By mixing various media, teachers can honor a child's values without debasing the learning process. There is room in intermedia for rock music, for audiovisual experiences — some of the things which really "grab" youngsters. Stifled, the subculture of the elementary school child fast becomes the counter-culture of the adolescent. If teachers are not aware enough to reach children in ways that can engage their attention and respect, a growing percentage of the youngsters will eventually find expression through drugs and violent or misguided social protest that could be destructive both to themselves and to society.

To this understanding of media as a means of connecting with youth I would also add the entire gamut of performing arts — dance, drama, music, and so forth — as being avenues of communication that are relatively unexplored because of their ambiguous position in the curriculum. Anyone who reads the newspapers should be able to see evidence of what happens when an affective generation attempts to throw off the excesses of a cognitively oriented culture.

Newton's new consciousness of media in its arts program began with the film animation classes at the Newton Creative Arts Center. Operating all summer and on Saturdays during the school year, the center gives youngsters a chance to get together with professionals — including Newton teachers of the arts — in fields that interest them. But because children won't choose to do something they don't know exists, I decided, as coordinator of the school arts program and center director, to add a film-maker to the corps of choreographers, composers, painters, drama directors, and others already at the center. The ensuing course developed in film-making was avidly accepted by the students, and its results created quite a bit of excitement when school art teachers viewed them at our first professional meeting the following fall.

I then set about to effect the change I felt was required to update the art program. Aside from the expected administrative and funding problems, there were attitudes that needed reshaping, even among teachers who were sympathetic to the idea in theory. Just as there are some who can't take the arts seriously as a part of general education, so there were art teachers in Newton who couldn't take media seriously as a respectable part of the art program. Gradually attitudes changed as we discussed new activities during workshops and informal meetings, and especially, as we observed what could be done with media during visits to production centers such as Intermedia Systems Corporation of Cambridge, and the intermedia presentations at Brandeis University and M.I.T.

Still there were teachers who rejected the ideas we encountered. Others couldn't find the energy to get rid of the obstacles that stood in the way of fresh programming, although they thought it was a good idea—for someone else. Then there were those who were curious and eager to work in media, and a few who had been using media prior to my arrival and who provided a nucleus of leadership.

Like most art teachers I have my own technological hangups and normally regard machines as cold, emotionless, intimidating devices. Yet the other day I heard my son exclaim of a Bolex movie camera that it "had soul." To me, machines are—or were—ends in themselves; to young people, they are objects that permit them to say something personal and unique in visual terms. And that, after all, is what art teachers seem to be harping about. The machine is basically a more sophisticated adjunct of the studio, and art teachers ought to be welcoming the light modulator as they formerly welcomed the collage as a harbinger of the avant-garde.

We may not feel comfortable watching our children do their homework to the accompaniment of TV and the telephone, yet obviously they are capable of juggling multiple modes of sensory input. As one writer put it, "Music, sounds, and pictures are part of their environment, much as the forests helped shape the imagery of the frontier child." In accepting the modes of communications which his elders have so conveniently provided, today's youngster moves with ease in situations where his control of technology permits experiences to become more emotionally real. In a sense, he has discovered that the machine may provide access to the heart.

"Art is anything you can get away with," says Marshall McLuhan. The Balinese put it in terms that are more acceptable to the art teacher: "We have no art. We do everything as best we can."

About all we can be sure of at this time in history is that if it works through the senses (primarily visual), if it calls for some degree of visual problem solving, if it elicits some sort of personal response from the levels of feeling and intellect, we may safely call it "art," at least in terms of the public schools. If we accept this definition we are as safe with a camera as with a box of crayons.

This definition is a natural one for young children. At Newton even first-graders are working directly on raw film and creating light images for projection. Children at the elementary level are fully capable of running tape recorders and film-sound projectors, handling cameras, or combining several modes of projection in the production of their own "light" shows.

The child employs media with his customary élan, and why shouldn't he? The camera is not a novelty to his family, and television has been his babysitter. He accepts condensed time-space concepts as he views live coverage of events; he accepts the fact that he can breakfast in one part of the world and lunch in another. In art, he would just as soon solve problems of structure perception, color, and design with photographic equipment and a dark room as he would with a box of crayons; the neat categories of art which are held in such esteem by his elders are so much academic quibbling to his avid multisensory curiosity.

In making the rounds in Newton last spring, I observed a number of activities brought about under the direction of art teachers who had accepted this definition of art and used media as a legitimate arm of their program. There is, for example, a new high school course called "Light," in which students design their own light modulators using mirrors, prisms, and intricate structures of balsa wood and theatrical gelatins. They also prepare light projects for other courses, such as slidetapes for social studies and English.

Another high school course entitled "The Hidden Landscape" deals with multisensory and environmental awareness. Here confrontation exercises, theater games, and activities designed to develop space awareness are taught with mapping exercises that chart the student's relationship to his neighborhood and community.

One junior high "light" treatment of *Alice in Wonderland* blends illustrations with abstract projections of many varieties and integrates them all with dramatic improvisation. While youngsters from the drama class enact scenes from Carroll's famous tale, the Mad Hatter and other loved characters dance, a la animation, across the back of the stage, juxtaposed with abstract figures.

The school where this production took place is a particularly difficult one since students represent the extreme economic polarities of the community. However, the new eighth-grade art program designed around light media has shown that youngsters of all social backgrounds have been able to work together in productive ways. After all, the new media are a part of the implicit curriculum they all hold in common.

Saturday morning classes in animation at the Newton Creative Arts Center have produced films on subjects such as war, social problems, and growing up. After several were shown on national TV networks and received awards from The Independent Film Makers Festival, they were purchased by Fordham University for its film library. The center's workshop, which is open to children in grades 6-12, covers such techniques as pixillation, cut-outs, flip cards, drawing on film, clay and puppet animation, montage, and collage.

Many art teachers at Newton share a concern with their colleagues in social studies for ways to make youngsters aware of how the quality of life is determined by the nature of one's surroundings. One junior high teacher feels the art program is as natural a place as any to begin and relies heavily upon media approaches. He has visited locations in Harlem, Reston, Va., and Columbia Point in Boston to gather material for slides, photo essays, and a set of film loops which he has created for both the art department and the social studies programs. His students go into their own neighborhoods with cameras. The slides and black-and-white photos that they feel are worth keeping are developed into prints, drawings, or paintings in the regular art program.

In like manner, an art and a history teacher have teamed together in a junior high school to work out a system whereby students visually debate an assigned topic. Each team researches its own material and presents its point of view through slides and sound tapes. The subject of the debate—the Civil War, for example—is then examined on stage and the rebuttals made verbally.

This year Newton has added a junior high photography course and has included film-making in the photography course of a senior high school. Another high school has added a humanities course fashioned around exploration of media and sensory awareness.

Students, for their part, are less interested in word games than in dealing with tools and ideas that have meaning for them. Thus, though some current efforts will be built upon past patterns of success, others undoubtedly will delight us through the element of surprise that one comes to expect of youngsters who are free to speak in their own language.

ANYONE CAN MAKE A FILMSTRIP **Richard Grillotti**

Yes! Anyone can make a filmstrip — easily, inexpensively, and quickly — without any experience or expensive photographic equipment.

Teachers often use 35mm filmstrips as a teaching device. Schools usually have several projectors floating around as well as a variety of filmstrips on almost every subject area. But, how many teachers have ever made their own filmstrips? How many teachers have utilized this process as an educational means of communication and learning?

Children are naturally curious about how things are made and what makes them tick. The making of a filmstrip is an ideal means of education through total group participation.

All one needs is a roll of 35mm clear or white movie leader and various color magic markers and felt tip pens. The leader comes in fifty foot rolls and costs only a few dollars. It can be purchased at any photo equipment dealer. The magic markers can be supplied by the children. If each child brought in one magic marker, the various colors could be shared by everyone.

The process itself involves drawing directly on the filmstrip with the magic markers. The size of each picture drawn should be approximately one inch by one inch (1x1 inch). If desired, a story line should be developed previous to the actual work. Commercially made filmstrips should be presented to the children for inspection — noting particularly the direction which the pictures face. (The tops and bottoms of each picture are adjacent to one another).

The filmstrip presented by my class was completed in two forty-five minute sittings by a group of 18 girls each responsible for the development of 24 inches of film, (about 15-20 frames). The girls arranged their desks so that the filmstrip was continuous. Upon completion the filmstrip was shown through a regular 35mm filmstrip projector. It was later used as part of an assembly program in conjunction with a discussion on color and abstract art.

Reprinted by permission of the author and Davis Publications from *School Arts* 69 (December 1969):12-13.

THE HAND-MADE SLIDE: WHETSTONE
FOR PERCEPTUAL ACUITY

Emily Scott

Film art, or making slides without a camera, lends itself easily to both large classes and small interest groups. Transparent colored gelatin, translucent tissues, and opqaue materials are arranged on acetate film, and lines are sketched directly on the film with plastic inks or a felt-tip pen. Gelatinous colors glow as the student overlays hue upon hue and then projects his creations upon a screen. The fascinating array of colors is startling and can be likened to the effect of a stained glass window.

This simple technique can be developed into a unique artistic experience which breaks down the resistant or inhibited student when he is confronted with the problem of "creating" something and is hesitant to take the initial step forward. Slide making is a painless way of opening avenues toward artistic expression and developing a student's perceptual acuity. Students look for, and respond to, color and form as they transform common "found" materials into delightful visual images.

Ruined color transparencies (both under- and over-exposed) can be readily adapted to this art form. Mounted slides can be scored with a razor blade or sharp edge, scorched with candle or match, and drawn upon with felt-tip markers, india ink, or pelikan acetate inks.

Clear film, thin acetate sheets, or bleached-out exposed film can be used by themselves or in combinations. As a suggestion, gelatin cut into ribbons or abstract shapes, and small objects such as threads, feathers, and netting can be stuck to the film and "sandwiched" by a second sheet of film. Also, gelatin sheets can be softened in water for several minutes, fastened to clear film backing, and further dissolved with brush and water. This creates a watercolor-like effect. If you prefer still another method, linear drawings on top or bottom surfaces, or on a second sheet of clear acetate, can be made with india inks or acrylic paints.

A projector, though not a necessity, is ideal to have on hand, for it encourages the student to evaluate, change, and re-evaluate his projected slide. Examining the bits of matter in the enlarged form, the student increases his capacity to make judgments about form, composition, texture, and *related* concepts.

As the student's excitement rises, he is forced to sustain his exercise in observation and response. Mood quality in the projected slide is a topic for discourse with other students. In the final composition, the student undergoes the critical review of other class members, whose interaction leads to the development of perceptual acuity.

Reprinted by permission of the author and *Arts & Activities* 71 (April 1972):30-31.

USING VISUAL MEDIA IN
MUSIC INSTRUCTION
Ruth Zinar

More and more visual aids are being made available to today's music teachers: TV, films, filmstrips, slides, transparencies, videotapes – the number and variety are impressive and almost overwhelming. For those who wonder whether all of these are of any real value and whether the concurrent involvement of the visual and the aural senses is really necessary for the learning process, recent research suggests that the creative and imaginative use of visual aids can be of distinct value in the music class.

In a study reported in 1975, Marjorie Evans Hoachlander[1] had one group of college students study for 45 minutes a selected chapter of the text *Ascent of Man* by Jacob Bronowsky. A second group saw a 45-minute video-cassette of the television version of the same chapter. In the post-test, results showed some advantage for the video-cassette instruction, implying that for some students, and in some situations, the use of moving illustrations intensifies the learning experience.

Another experiment by Jerry Randolph Hill[2] compared a conventional teaching approach and the use of filmstrips in the teaching of music appreciation at the college level (ie: a unit on "Elements of Music"). Although in most aspects achievement of both groups was equal, in the subtest on melody recognition the experimental group did score significantly higher than the control group.

Neither the attitudes of the students towards the course nor their liking for the music was considered in either of these studies; but in very recent research, the affective responses of elementary school children to several types of TV presentations was explored.[3] Mjung Ja Nam developed programs to illustrate Bach's "Minuet in G." One showed a musician playing the work on a harpsichord. Another used abstract paper cut-out animation with "structural matching" of the music; and a third used "tonal matching" – pictures of children that could be matched with the mood of the music. In addition, a short videotape was shown giving information about the life of Bach.

A recording of the work was played for the children and they were given a test to determine their feelings about the music. Additional tests were given following the TV programs. Almost all of the children responded correctly to questions about Bach's life. The visualized versions of the composition were much more meaningful and enjoyable to these fifth- and sixth-grade children than just listening to the music.

The favorite part of the program was the animation, the harpsichord performance was second, and the "tonal matching" was third. Obviously, not only did a visual presentation enhance the children's appreciation of the music, but it was the animation – the most imaginative and creative visualization – which was the most attractive to them.

Reprinted by permission of the author and *American Music Teacher* 28 (April 1979):20, 22.

Paul A. Haack reached similar conclusions[4] regarding the effectiveness of visual aids in teaching musical concepts. In his experiment, two groups of Junior High School pupils were randomly selected and placed in Music Appreciation classes. The curriculum of both sections was devoted to music of the Classical and Romantic eras. In the experimental classes, "general ideals" of eighteenth-century European Classicism were contrasted with "Romantic tendencies," with art and music examples presented for each style. The art examples were not used in the control group's classes.

In the post-test in which musical excerpts were to be classified as Romantic or Classical, the experimental group "demonstrated significant superiority in the ... achievement of the broad musical concepts ... in spite of less actual time"[5] spent listening. The "bisensory approach," Haack concludes, "is the more effective one for the development of the aural concepts and skills under surveillance."[6]

There are a number of possible reasons for the benefits of visual aids in a music class. The variety of presentation keeps motivation high, attracts attention, and reawakens interest. As a result, pupils become more involved in what is being taught. The visual aid can make abstract ideas more concrete, and hence easier to grasp and to remember. Art and music, the visual and the aural, are expressions of the same kinds of experiences, ideas, and emotions, and are similar in spite of using different media. For these reasons, it is certainly possible that using "the visual ... may enhance the aural perception and understanding of music.... "[7]

There are many possible ways that a music teacher can easily enrich and enhance music classes through the use of visuals.

Imagine that you are going to teach via a TV program. You can understand how dull it would be to the viewers to have the camera focused on you all the time. If you challenge yourself to provide the "visuals" to illustrate the abstract ideas and concepts, you will be well on the way to making lectures and explanations more vivid, more concrete, more interesting, and more enjoyable.

For example, "transparencies," plastic film upon which a diagram or picture is placed—by manufacturers via a highly sophisticated chemical process, or else drawn on by the instructor using grease pencils or special marking pens, then projected onto a screen via the overhead projector—can be used to great advantage in a number of ways.

Stories can be sketched to illustrate the events depicted in program music. Transparencies with "overlays" (additional transparencies to be placed on top of an original basic film) can show the basics of pitch notation, development of major and minor scales and chords, changing rhythms, or the concept of variations. Many of these transparencies are available or they can be made by students or teacher. This can be done by starting with a basic transparency showing the staff with the overlays illustrating leger lines, key signatures, the names of lines or spaces, or other theory concepts.

An instructor can run exercises for analysis or student theory homework through the "Thermofax" copying machine, using a special plastic film. In seconds, a perfect, permanent copy emerges. Then, with the use of special washable transparency markers, corrections can be made, changes added, discussed, and indicated directly on the transparency while it is projected in a lighted room. All the time, the teacher faces the class, ready to ask and answer questions and to evoke discussion.

Original student instrumentations and chamber-music compositions can be copies via Thermofax onto a transparency film. The other students can then "try out" or play the composition. Arduous and time-consuming copying of the scores is made unnecessary. Similarly, transparencies can be prepared ahead of time. It is not necessary to take up class time putting theory examples, or songs, on the board. Some music teachers have, with great success, prepared transparencies with words of songs typed, using a special typewriter with large block letters. Projected onto the screen during assembly periods, everyone can see the words. Costly duplication and wasted time handing out song sheets are eliminated. Everything but the "bouncing ball" is ready for the pupils following the projected words.

A large number of attractive audio-filmstrips are available combining recordings (or cassettes) and pictures illustrating music history, ethnic music, program music, or musical instruments. These are adapted for use on all levels from kindergarten through college. It is, however, important to preview them to make sure that the filmstrips are suitable for the age group and appropriate for the subject matter. These filmstrips are convenient and flexible, being appropriate for individualized study or for large groups and easy to handle, use, and store. They are not very expensive when one compares their cost to collections of prints and books with similar pictures. In addition, student participation can be encouraged by having pupils work the projector or by assigning all or part of the class to take notes on special parts. Obviously, discussion and questions should be part of the lesson in which filmstrips are used.

The filmstrips which are automatically synchronized with the music have the advantage over those which use "beeps" to indicate the time to change to the next frame. The "beeps" are distracting, especially when they are "offkey." Fortunately, more and more projectors and filmstrips for automatic synchronization are being made available.

The numerous films available to the music teacher can not only help to enrich and enhance music appreciation and music history courses; but for some pupils, they provide the kind of learning experiences required by them for best results. For a generation of children brought up with television, the multi-sense appeal of pictures with sound and movement has become the learning mode to which they best respond.

Prepared charts, pictures, and diagrams, if these are large enough to be seen without projection, attractive enough, and clearly illustrative of the concept being taught, are also extremely valuable. Haack's study showed how art can increase understanding of musical style. The same is true of musical form, where diagrams can illuminate concepts such as ABA, Theme and Variations, Fugue, or Sonata Allegro.

It is not easy or quick to develop a resource file of pictures, drawings, paintings, sketches, cartoons, charts, posters, models, and diagrams of composers, instruments, historical styles, theory concepts, etc., but constant alertness as you thumb through magazines, journals, newspapers and advertising brochures can be rewarding. (One of the most beautiful illustrations I have is a very large reproduction, in color, of a medieval music manuscript, mounted and laminated. It was cut out of giftwrap paper at Christmas time.)

There are so many resources for teaching music and so many more can be created. In an age of mass media, the teacher can no longer simply lecture and "impart" information. If "the media is the message," then the message of using visual media to enhance, enrich, and explain the abstract aural concepts of music is that Man's expressions take a variety of forms and that these forms can express a commonality of human experience.

Footnotes

[1]Marjorie Evans Hoachlander, "Book in Motion, Book in Print," (unpublished doctoral dissertation, University of Maryland, 1975).

[2]Jerry Randolph Hill, "An Investigation and Evaluation of the Use of Visual Aids for Teaching Music Appreciation at the College Level," (unpublished doctoral dissertation, University of Oklahoma, 1972).

[3]Mjung Ja Nam, "Development of an Instructional Television Program That Seeks to Discover Whether or Not Visual Images Facilitate Classical Music Appreciation," (unpublished doctoral dissertation, University of Oregon, 1976).

[4]Paul A. Haack, "A Study Involving the Visual Arts in the Development of Musical Concepts," *Journal of Research in Music Education* XVIII, 4, Winter, 1970, pp. 393-398.

[5]*Ibid.*, p. 397.

[6]*Ibid.*

[7]Haack, *Ibid.*

POPULAR MUSIC: A CREATIVE
TEACHING RESOURCE

B. Lee Cooper

Many people question the value of listening to, let alone studying, popular songs. Their doubts are usually based on several surface observations related to contemporary music. The volume of many recordings is deafening; the lyrics of some songs seem repetitive and unimaginative; and disc jockeys who scream jingles, blow horns, or heap senseless praise on tunes which are here today and gone tomorrow are annoying. Yet during the past decade a variety of scholars — musical theorists, psychologists, cultural historians, teachers of poetry and literature, sociologists, and linguists — have begun to carefully examine the nature and meaning of popular music. This serious study is not just a quirk. It marks an attempt to understand the reason for the immense popularity of contemporary singers, songwriters, and their songs.

Although experts on popular music disagree on many issues, there is consensus among them that the music of today is notably different from music produced during any other period in history. There are three reasons for this. First, the commercial distribution and radio broadcasting of popular recordings has created a vast listening public which is constantly exposed to new tunes in cars, homes, elevators, and department stores. The popular song is a universally available phenomenon. Second, technological advancements in musical instruments and other sound-producing equipment (tape recorders, speakers, and amplifiers) have enabled singers to produce such high quality recording material that, as a recent audiocassette advertisement declares, "You can't tell whether it's Ella Fitzgerald (live) or Memorex." Finally, the quality of song lyrics has increased so dramatically that many English teachers refer to popular songwriters such as Bob Dylan, Paul Simon, Carole King, Don McLean, and Paul McCartney as "poets."

But while the lyrics of some contemporary songs have been richly praised as poetry, the words of other popular tunes have been condemned by politicians, theologians, and journalists as sinister propaganda tools. The fact that modern singers, unlike their pre-1960 predecessors, tend to deal lyrically with controversial social and personal issues has created concern about the influence of popular music. Antiwar chants, religious tunes, women's liberation melodies, and social protest songs have been used to depict the image of the United States through lyrical means. It is this descriptive aspect of contemporary music which is valuable to teachers.

What Is Popular Music?

The broad field of popular music is usually described by dividing it into categories of songs or singing styles. Commentators frequently use terms such as

Reprinted by permission of the author and the Association for Educational Communications and Technology from *Audiovisual Instruction* 24 (March 1979):37-43.

"blues," "rock," "jazz," "country," "folk," "rhythm and blues," "pop," "bluegrass," and "soul" to delineate types of modern music. Each of these terms has an element of validity; yet each category is potentially misleading. The real problem begins when a student of popular music attempts to classify the style of such versatile singers as Elvis Presley, Ray Charles, or Barbra Streisand. The fact that these three artists perform songs in a variety of styles creates classification confusion. Of course, the task of defining the performing styles of Johnny Cash, B. B. King, Phil Ochs, Pete Seeger, or the Archies is much easier.

To avoid this type of stylistic dilemma, the general term "popular music" used in this article describes those songs which have attained public acceptance as has been noted quantitatively in music publications such as *Billboard* and *Cashbox*. Most songs mentioned in the following pages have been listed in the "Top 100" charts of these two musical digests during the past twenty-five years. The idea that a song is popular means that it is played frequently in public places—at dances, in juke boxes at restaurants, on radios, or anywhere else people gather.

When social studies students examine popular music, the elements of melody, rhythm, harmony, acoustics and form are of secondary importance to the content of a song's lyrics. This does not mean that instrumental performances are of no significance as popular music. However, the learning potential of a modern song is most often found in the quality of the verbal message which is delivered through the lyrics which a singer articulates. Content creates images. The image of a society depicted in a song frequently exerts a stronger hold on a listener than the social reality which surrounds him. That is, songs of love, peace, and joy can create a sense of well-being in an individual's mind even though he or she may be suffering from personal or social problems. Likewise, songs may challenge the status quo in order to stimulate the notion in the public mind that things aren't going so well. The lyrics written by Stephen Stills and performed by the Buffalo Springfield illustrate this latter point.

> There's a man with a gun over there,
> What it is ain't exactly clear.
> There's a man with a gun over There,
> Tellin' me I've got to beware.
> It's time we stop, children,
> What's that sound?
> Everybody look what's goin' down.
> —"For What It's Worth"

Why Use Popular Music in Social Studies Classes?

Social studies instruction should culminate in the ability of a student to anticipate, understand, direct, evaluate, and live with constant social change. Most historians agree that the only thing that is less stable than man's interpretation of the past is his ability to objectively comprehend changing events of his own lifetime. The study of contemporary society demands that both the teacher and the student acknowledge their myopic tendencies and actively seek new methods and materials for investigating shifts and alterations in present-day life.

One potentially beneficial resource for analyzing the causes and effects of social change is the medium of popular music. If a social studies teacher is seeking to test his students' abilities in using skills such as problem identification, information gathering, hypothesis-formulating, and decision-making, then the use of popular music should provide a rich field for classroom experimentation.

The image of American society in contemporary lyrics is complex. While some songs praise patriotism ("Okee from Muskogee"), others condemn blind public support of military endeavors ("Fortunate Son"). A few songs seem to support the pleasures of drug use ("White Rabbit"), while other lyrics condemn the sale of narcotics ("The Pusher"), and stress the deadly effects of speed and cocaine ("Amphetamine Annie" and "Snowblind Friend"). Thus, the paradoxes of American society are accurately mirrored in the lyrics of contemporary songs.

This type of thematic structure can be easily expanded to illustrate various specific points of social, political, or economic concern. For instance, youth's traditionally ambivalent attitude toward material goods can be dramatically demonstrated by contrasting Barret Strong's assertation, "Gimme money! That's all I want!" ("Money") with the lyrical warning by the O'Jays, "Money can drive some people out of their minds!" ("For the Love of Money").

One strength of this teaching approach is its flexibility. An instructor may approach a universally relevant concept such as "materialism" from a variety of perspectives based upon the specific recordings employed. Once such a theme has been identified, some members of the class will inevitably attempt to outdo the teacher in assembling their own audio references. Thus, the original two-song dichotomy on materialism—Barret Strong vs. The O'Jays—may be expanded through student suggestions to include "Busted" by Ray Charles, "Money Honey" by the Drifters, "Spanish Harlem" by Ben K. King, "Patches" by Clarence Carter, and "Payin' the Cost to Be the Boss" by B. B. King. Although this open-ended approach may initially disrupt controlled, preplanned class presentations, the enthusiasm generated among the students will more than compensate for occasional problems created by expanding the time assigned to a specific topic.

Where Can Resources on Teaching Popular Music Be Obtained?

The use of popular music in the classroom has not received much academic commentary. Likewise, the ability of librarians to adapt to the needs of social studies teachers and students in terms of securing and utilizing contemporary recordings has not been encouraging. The articles cited in "Teaching Approaches Using Popular Music" (see Figure 1) will be helpful resources for developing practical classroom strategies.

Another question which invariably arises during any discussion concerning the use of popular music is: "Where can the lyrics for contemporary songs be obtained?" No social studies teacher can be expected to feel comfortable with a medium as strange and new as popular recordings. However, this initial insecurity can be beneficial for stimulating professional growth. It can also enable students to assume the roles of "the expert" in terms of providing non-traditional learning resources for classroom investigation. Aside from relying on student good will, teachers will be pleased to discover that lyric collections are readily available at reasonable paperback rates (see Figure 2).

Figure 1

Teaching Approaches Using Popular Music

Patricia Averill, "How To Teach The Rock and Roll Generation What They Don't Want To Hear," *Popular Culture Methods*, III (Spring 1976), pp. 31-36.

Roger L. Brown and Michael O'Leary, "Pop Music in an English Secondary School System." *American Behavioral Scientist*, XIV (January/February 1971), pp. 401-413.

B. Lee Cooper, "Chuck Berry's Golden Decade ... ," *The History Teacher*, VIII (Feburary 1975), pp. 300-301.

_____. "Exploring the Future Through Popular Music," *Media and Methods*, XII (April 1976), pp. 32-35ff.

David Difty and John Anthony Scott, "How To Use Folk Songs." Washington, D.C.: National Council for the Social Studies, 1969.

David Feldman, "How To Teach Students About Something They Already Know More About Than You Do: Some Approaches To Teaching Rock Music," *Popular Culture Methods*, III (Spring 1976), pp. 22-31.

David S. Linton, "Rock and the Media," *Media and Methods*, XIII (October 1976), pp. 56-59.

Anne W. Lyons, "Creative Teaching in Interdisciplinary Humanities: The Human Values in Pop Music," *Minnesota English Journal*, (Winter 1974), pp. 23-31.

David E. Morse, "Avant-Rock in the Classroom," *English Journal*, LVIII (February 1969), pp. 196-200ff.

Harold F. Mosher, Jr., "The Lyrics of American Pop Music: A New Poetry," *Popular Music and Society*, I (Spring 1972), pp. 167-176.

Charles Seeger, "Folk Music in the Schools of a Highly Industrialized Society," in *The American Folk Scene: Dimensions of the Folksong Revival*, edited by David A. DeTurk and A. Poulin, Jr. (New York: Dell Publishing Company, Inc., 1967), pp. 88-94.

Figure 2

Paperback Resources for Popular Music Lyrics

Alan Aldridge (ed.). *The Beatles Illustrated Lyrics*. New York: Delacorte Press, 1969.

_____ (ed.). *The Beatles Illustrated Lyrics—2*. New York: Delacorte Press, 1971.

Best Songs. Derby, Connecticut: Charlton Publications, Inc., 1941-1977.

Bruce L. Chipman (comp.). *Hardening Rock: An Organic Anthology of the Adolescence of Rock 'N Roll*. Boston: Little Brown and Company, 1972.

Richard Goldstein (ed.). *The Poetry of Rock*. New York: Bantam Books, Inc., 1969.

Barbara Farris Graves and Donald J. McBain (eds.). *Lyric Voices: Approaches to the Poetry of Contemporary Song*. New York: John Wiley and Sons, Inc., 1972.

Hit Parader. Derby, Connecticut: Charlton Publications, Inc., 1941-1977.

The Motown Era. New York: Grosset and Dunlap, Inc., 1971.

A. X. Nicholas (ed.). *The Poetry of Soul*. New York: Bantam Books, Inc., 1971.

_____ (ed.). *Woke Up This Morning': Poetry of the Blues*. New York: Bantam Books, Inc., 1973.

Milton Okun (comp.). *Great Songs ... of the Sixties*. Chicago: Quadrangle Books, 1970.

David R. Pichaske (ed.). *Beowulf To Beatles: Approaches To Poetry*. New York: Free Press, 1972.

Rock and Soul Songs. Derby, Connecticut: Charlton Publications, Inc., 1955-1977.

Song Hits Magazine. Derby, Connecticut: Charlton Publications, Inc., 1936-1977.

Stephanie Spinner (ed.). *Rock is Beautiful: An Anthology of American Lyrics, 1953-1968*. New York: Dell Publishing Company, Inc., 1970.

How Can a Social Studies Teacher Introduce Popular Music Resources?

Rather than continuing to outline the theory of using popular music in the social studies classroom, the following pages provide a series of specific teaching strategies which can be employed to motivate student interest. Each recommended instructional unit is thematically organized and headed by a specific question for reflective consideration, along with a set of six to ten concepts which are directly related to each theme. They are also supported by two types of teaching resources — popular music recordings and textbook readings — which have been selected to illustrate the theme and to spark student interest, imagination, and creativity.

Technological Revolution

Question for Reflective Consideration:
"How has the technological revolution in electronic equipment during the past thirty years altered the American music industry?"

Concepts/Issues to be Investigated:

microphones	recording techniques	quadrophonics
amplification	stereophonic sound	speakers
earphones	turntables	tape quality
	accoustic guitar	fidelity

Instructional Strategy:

Have each student develop a list of technological advancements which have influenced the production of contemporary music. Invite a music teacher and a physics instructor to serve as guest lecturers and discussion leaders on the related topics of "New Sounds" and "New Sound-Making Devices." Also invite members of a local rock band to demonstrate their craft and to illustrate the sound variations between electronic and non-electronic instruments.

Songs and Performers:

Acoustic Versus Electronic Sound by an Artist

Muddy Waters, "Hoochie Coochie Man" (from *Heavy Heads*, Chess Records, LPS-1522)
Muddy Waters, "Hoochie Coochie Man" (from *Electric Mud*, Cadet Concept, LPS-314)

Unique Sounds on Records

The Beach Boys, "Good Vibrations"
Tommy James and the Shondells, "Mirage"

Cut-and-Paste Comedy Recordings

Dixie Goodman, "Mr. Jaws"
Buchanan and Goodman, "Flying Saucer"

Amplified Remakes of Traditional Hits

"Please Mr. Postman" The Marvelettes (Tamla Records — 1961)
  The Carpenters (A & M Records — 1974)

"Pledging My Love"	Johnny Ace (Duke Records—1955)
	Elvis Presley (RCA Records—1977)
"Rock and Roll Music"	Chuck Berry (Chess Records—1957)
	The Beach Boys (Brother/Reprise Records—1976)
"Roll Over Beethoven"	Chuck Berry (Chess Records—1956)
	The Electric Light Orchestra (United Artists—1973)
"Since I Met You Baby"	Ivory Joe Hunter (Atlantic Records—1956)
	Freddy Fender (GRT Records—1975)

Reading Resources:

Ivan Berger, "One Hundred Years of Recording," *Stereo Review*, XXXIX (July 1977), pp. 62-65.

Richard Robinson, *Electronic Rock: The Rock Musicians' Guide to Guitars and Amplifiers*. New York: Pyramid Books, 1971.

C. A. Schicke, *Revolution in Sound: A Biography of the Recording Industry*. Boston: Little, Brown and Company, 1974.

Graham Vulliamy and Ed Lee (eds.), *Pop Music in School*. London: Cambridge University Press, 1976.

Herbert H. Wise (ed.), *Professional Rock and Roll: A Complete Guide to the Electric Band*. New York: Collier Books, 1967.

Historical Images

Question for Reflective Consideration:

"How accurate are popular singers and songwriters in their depiction of prominent historical events?"

Concepts/Issues to be Investigated:

causation	interpretations	myths
facts	propaganda	images
balladeer	stereotypes	heroes

Instructional Approach:

Have students discuss the oral history found in traditional ballads which praised the heroic deeds of Robin Hood and John Henry or condemned big business' hostility toward unionism ("Joe Hill") in 19th century America. Then ask the class to reflect on the historical accuracy of the stories presented in the following songs.

Records and Performers:

Historical Topic	*Popular Music Resource*
The Battle of New Orleans	Johnny Horton, "The Battle of New Orleans"
A Civil War Incident	Joan Baez, "The Night They Drove Old Dixie Down"
Labor Problems in Coal Mining Communities	Tennessee Ernie Ford, "Sixteen Tons"

John F. Kennedy During World War II	Jimmy Dean, "P.T. 109"
The Assassinations of Abraham Lincoln, Martin Luther King, Jr., and John F. Kennedy	Dion, "Abraham, Martin, and John"
The Assassination of John F. Kennedy	Tommy Cash, "Six White Horses"
The Valor of Vietnam Soldiers	Barry Sadler, "The Ballad of the Green Berets"
The Kent State Incident	Crosby, Stills, Nash and Young, "Ohio"
The Trial of the "Chicago 7"	Crosby, Stills, Nash and Young, "Chicago"

Reading Resources:

B. Lee Cooper, "Oral History, Popular Music, and Les McCann," *Social Studies* LXVII (May/June 1976), pp. 115-118.

R. Serge Denisoff, *Sing a Song of Social Significance.* Bowling Green, Ohio: Bowling Green University Popular Press, 1972.

Harris Friedburg, "Bob Dylan: Psychohistorian of a Generation," *The Chronicle of Higher Education*, VIII (January 28, 1974), pp. 15-16.

Richard A. Rosenstone, "The Times They Are A-Changin': The Music of Protest," The Annals of the American Academy of Political and Social Science, LXXXII (May 1969), pp. 131-144.

Social Mobility

Question for Reflective Consideration:

"How does popular music depict routes toward upward social mobility and personal independence for Americans?"

Concepts/Issues to be Investigated:

social mobility	education	success
equal opportunity	materialism	access
Horatio Alger	self-made man	democracy

Instructional Approach:

Explain the rags-to-riches, Horatio Alger theme which dominated the minds of upwardly mobile Americans during the late 19th and early 20th century. Ask students to consider the types of personal goals and aspirations which are found in the lyrics of the following contemporary songs.

Songs and Performers:

Lou Rawls, "Dead End Street"
The Drifters, "On Broadway"
Chuck Berry, "Johnny B. Goode"
The Impressions, "Keep On Pushin' "
Frank Sinatra, "My Way"

Jim Croce, "I Got A Name"
Rascals, "People Gotta Be Free"
Sammy Davis, Jr., "I've Got To Be Me"
Lou Rawls, "A Natural Man"
The Monkees, "(I'm Not Your) Steppin' Stone"

Reading Resources:

"Ray Charles—Playboy Interview," *Playboy*, XVII (March 1970), pp. 67-82.

Phyl Garland, "Roberta Flack: New Musical Messenger," *Ebony*, XXVI (January 1971), pp. 54-62.

Steve Glazier, "Richie Havens: From Brooklyn To the Other Side of the Universe" (July 20, 1968), in *The Rolling Stone Rock 'N' Roll Reader*, edited by Ben Fong-Torres (New York: Bantam Books, Inc., 1974), pp. 282-284.

Ivan D. Illich, *Celebration of Awareness*. Garden City, New York: Doubleday and Company, Inc., 1971.

David Morse, *Motown and the Arrival of Black Music*. New York: Collier Books, 1971.

Social Criticism

Question for Reflective Consideration:

"Why have the writers and singers of popular songs elected to emphasize controversial social and political topics in their lyrics?"

Concepts/Issues to be Investigated:

controversial issues	ecology	drug abuse
race relations	war	politics
social criticism	democracy	muckraking

Instructional Approach:

Have each student assemble a list of four to six songs which illustrate varying points of view on a significant issue of social or political concern.

Records and Performers:

Drug Abuse
Steppenwolf, "The Pusher"
Jefferson Airplane, "White Rabbit"
Canned Heat, "Amphetamine Annie"
The Association, "Along Comes Mary"
Paul Revere and the Raiders, "Kicks"
The Jimi Hendrix Experience, "Purple Haze"
The Rolling Stones, "Mother's Little Helper"

International Conflicts
Bob Seeger System, "2 + 2 = ?"
Country Joe and the Fish, "I-Feel-Like-I'm-Fixin'-to-Die Rag"
Barry Sadler, "Ballad of the Green Berets"
Edwin Starr, "War"
Phil Ochs, "I Ain't Marching Anymore"
Leon Russell, "Give Peace a Chance"
Bob Dylan, "Masters of War"

Race

Elvis Presley, "In The Ghetto"
James Brown, "Say It Loud – I'm
   Black and I'm Proud"
Neil Young, "Southern Man"
The Impressions, "Choice of Color"
Curtis Mayfield, "Mighty Mighty,
   Spade and Whitey"
Sly and the Family Stone, "Don't
   Call Me Nigger, Whitey"
The Rolling Stones, "Brown Sugar"

Environmental Protection

Marvin Gaye, "Mercy, Mercy Me
   (The Ecology)"
The Monkees, "Pleasant Valley
   Sunday"
Three Dog Night, "The Family of
   Man"
Marvin Gaye, "Inner City Blues
   (Make Me Wanna Holler)"
Tom Paxton, "Whose Garden Was
   This?"
Cat Stevens, "Where Do the Chil-
   dren Play?"
Joni Mitchell, "Big Yellow Taxi"
Tom Lehrer, "Pollution"
Stephen Stills, "Ecology Song"

Reading Resources:

Leon Bramson and George W. Geothals (eds.), *War: Studies From Psychology,
   Sociology, and Anthropology.* New York: Basic Books, 1964.
R. Serge Denisoff, "Folk-Rock: Folk Music, Protest, or Commercialism?"
   Journal of Popular Culture, III (Fall, 1969), pp. 214-230.
Robert Detweiler, John N. Sutherland, and Michael S. Werthmau (eds.), *Envi-
   ronmental Decay In Its Historical Context.* Glenview, Illinois: Scott, Fores-
   man and Company, 1973.
Jonathan Eisen (ed.), *The Age of Rock: Sounds of the American Cultural Revo-
   lution.* New York: Vintage Books, 1969.
_____ (ed.), *The Age of Rock – 2: Sights and Sounds of the American
   Cultural Revolution.* New York: Vintage Books, 1970.
Joel Fort, *The Pleasure Seekers: The Drug Crisis, Youth, and Society.* Indianapolis: Bobbs-Merrill Book Company, 1969.

Women's Movement

Question for Reflective Consideration:

"Has the rise of the female superstar in popular music positively affected the
status of the women's movement in the United States?"

Concepts/Issues to be Investigated:

sexism	affirmative action	ERA
discrimination	equal opportunity	liberation
awareness	political influence	identity

Instructional Approach:

Have the class construct a list of contemporary female singing stars. Assign
three students as a research team to investigate a female singer's personal
background, the history of her recording success, and the social and political
themes which can be found in her songs. In addition to the singers listed below,
include: Buffy Sainte-Marie, Joni Mitchell, Peggy Lee, Carole King, Karen

Carpenter, Bonnie Bramlett, Janis Joplin, Roberta Flack, Mary Travers, Toni Tennile, Marie Osmond, Bette Midler, Barbra Streisand, and Natalie Cole.

Records and Performers:

Liberation
The Stone Poneys, "Different Drum"
Helen Reddy, "I Am Woman"

Male Chauvinism
Linda Ronstadt, "When Will I Be Loved"
Carly Simon, "You're So Vain"
The Marvellettes, "Playboy"

Sexual Responsibility
Jean Knight, "Mr. Big Stuff"
Diana Ross and the Supremes, "Love Child"

Social Commentary
Joan Baez, "With God On Our Side"
Joni Mitchell, "Big Yellow Taxi"

Male-Female Relations
Janis Joplin, "Me and Bobby McGee"
Aretha Franklin, "Respect"
Gladys Knight and the Pips, "I Heard It Through the Grapevine"

Reading Resources:

Joan Baez, *Daybreak*. New York: Avon Books, 1969.

Robb Baker. *Bette Midler*. New York: Popular Library, 1975.

Noel Coppage, "Joni Mitchell: Innocence on a Spree," *Stereo Review*, XXXVI (April 1976), pp. 64-67.

_____. "Country Music's Traipsin' Women," *Stereo Review*, XXXIII (December 1974), pp. 84-89.

Phyl Garland, "Roberta Flack: New Musical Messenger," *Ebony*, XXVI (January 1971), pp. 54-62.

Deborah Landau. *Janis Joplin: Her Life and Times*. New York: Paperback Library, 1971.

Charles Morse and Ann Morse. *Carly Simon*. Mankato, Minnesota: Creative Educational Society, Inc., 1974.

James T. Olsen, *Aretha Franklin*. Mankato, Minnesota: Creative Educational Society, Inc., 1974.

Earl Paige *et al.* "Diana: A Billboard Special Supplement," *Billboard* Magazine, (March 20, 1976), pp. 1-72.

Jerome L. Rodnitzky, "Songs of Sisterhood: The Music of Women's Liberation," *Popular Music and Society*, IV (1975), pp. 77-85.

William A. Sievert, "For Every Bob Dylan, A Joni Mitchell," *The Chronicle of Higher Education*, XI (January 12, 1976), p. 17.

Jerry Silverman (comp.). *The Liberated Woman's Songbook*. New York: Collier Books, 1971.

Robert Windeler, "Carole King: 'You Can Get To Know Me Through My Music'," *Stereo Review*, XXX (May 1973), pp. 76-77.

V

INDUSTRIAL/VOCATIONAL EDUCATION

Courses available in the areas of industrial and vocational education consist of subject matter that will prepare the young adult to compete in the job market soon after high school graduation. Typically industrial and vocational settings in the real world work with secondary teachers in this area to provide a contact with current developments in industry and at times, offer financial support for appropriate classroom-laboratory experiences.

The use of nonprint in both areas is vitally important if students are to compete in the modern industrial marketplace. In "The Industrial Arts Teacher and the Media Specialist," Gordon E. Martin speaks to the importance of coordinating instructional planning between the media specialist and the industrial arts instructor. The author cites examples of how students and a media specialist can work cooperatively to fulfill stated objectives in involving visual productions and a variety of instructional tasks. Joe Kaiser in "AV Can Be a Teacher's Biggest Help" reiterates the contribution that nonprint in his classroom makes in the transmittance of facts and the demonstration of manual operations. He also explains how the teacher should go about planning and utilizing audiovisual materials in the classroom. The final article in this section by Ralph R. Bush demonstrates a unique way of individualizing instruction through learning packages in a shop setting. The 18 safety lessons are contained in photo-notebooks with an accompanying audiocassette tape either in English or Spanish for those students who have missed the basic instruction or who wish a review.

THE INDUSTRIAL ARTS TEACHER
AND THE MEDIA SPECIALIST

Gordon E. Martin

Industrial arts deals with industry—its organization, materials, occupations, processes, and products—and with the problems resulting from today's technological society. The task of the industrial arts teacher—to interpret industry when industry is changing at an ever-increasing rate—is a most demanding one.

To carry out this task, the classroom teacher needs a better understanding of the benefits of employing educational media, and there needs to be a closer working relationship between the specialist in *media* and the classroom teacher, who is a specialist in *content*.

This is true at the most basic level. Scobey (1972) notes that students in elementary school industrial arts programs need first-hand experiences with such areas as the multimedia center. This does not mean that the teachers are to show an abundance of films, slides, and filmstrips about contemporary materials, tools, and processes. Instead, the media specialists should work directly with the students in independent activities in which they develop their own materials. The media specialist might help with layout, lettering and coloring a visual display; and by suggesting maps, and other materials that students might use. By creating such educational materials, the student becomes acquainted with industrial sites and processes that are impractical to experience directly.

Media and Industrial Arts at the Secondary Level

At the secondary level, instructional technology has an ever-increasing part to play in the industrial arts program. For example, Maley (1969), describing a contemporary junior high school industrial arts program, identified as a general goal for one lesson: "To develop the student's *knowledge* and *understanding* about the organization of the management personnel in industry" (p. 96). Two of the nine behavioral objectives to fulfill this goal involve the development of visual aids.

One objective states: "The student will develop a photographic display of the student personnel organization" (p. 96). This objective will require the assistance of the media specialist to help students make a visual chart requiring them to deal with size, color, spacing, balance, and effectiveness.

In realizing these objectives, the media specialist and the content specialist cooperate to meet the stated goals. The media specialist is able to recommend specific types of hardware and software that lend themselves to a particular objective. If a specific task does not involve motion, the instructor in media may recommend a slide/cassette format for such a program; if motion is vital to the

Reprinted by permission of the author and the Association for Educational Communications and Technology from *Audiovisual Instruction* 21 (April 1976):36-38.

concepts, then video cassettes, Super 8mm sound or silent film, or some other format may be used.

Assistance related to the *proper use* of visual media should be of major concern to the media specialist. For example, another behavioral objective related to the original goal states: "The *student* will *use* an organization chart in the directing of a line production experience or major industry study (p. 96)." The objective implies that media specialists can assist the student in using the chart properly. This aid can take several approaches — how to hold a chart in front of an audience, how to emphasize data on a chart, how to speak in front of a group using a visual aid, etc.

One commonly accepted approach to the interpretation of industry is to have the students look first at those elements that are basic to all humankind. These elements would include study of tools and machines, power and energy, communications and transportation. The entire class would choose one element and then conduct a major study of a number of events within the element.

Assume the class chose to conduct a unit study in the area of communications and transportation. A class of 30 students would produce 30 different projects depicting the development of humankind in the area of communications and transportation. These projects might include scale models researched and constructed by the students. Projects might include models of a street car, covered wagon, early typewriter, early telephone, or covered bridge. The end product is the accumulation of 30 different projects illustrating the growth and development of communications and transportation.

Some secondary industrial arts programs look into future problems that might face mankind. Typical problems could include housing, transportation, and water and air pollution. In a typical unit of study reflecting a major problem of the future — transportation — students constructed a model of a space shuttle system.

In such secondary school programs, students constructed three-dimensional models instead of the traditional, bulky industrial arts project. While one of the roles of the industrial arts teacher requires expertise in full-scale construction techniques, the role of the media specialist might require expertise in good model development.

The media specialist could help students to accomplish a variety of tasks:

- Determine the proper scale for the model so that it could be displayed in front of a class.
- Identify and choose good quality model materials.
- Make and apply the proper graphics for the model.
- Show the value of models as a communications medium.
- Make a transparency to aid the student's explanation of the project.
- Make and develop slides for use in classroom discussion.
- Making and developing photographs of other models that have been commercially constructed.
- Use a model properly as a communication tool in class discussion.
- Identify reference books about model making.

Educational Media in Teacher Training Programs

College level industrial arts programs emphasize the teacher-training aspects related to the interpretation of industry with little emphasis on educational media as a teaching method. Traditionally, educational media courses have been offered to all disciplines in a single setting. Because of the unique environment in which industrial arts programs operate and the availability of tools, machines, and equipment to the students as well as the teacher, cooperation between industrial arts teacher training programs and the media specialist and the media center is particularly desirable. In many instances across the nation (and not peculiar to industrial arts), it is possible for a student to graduate and become employed as a teacher without ever taking an educational media course. Yet, the value and importance of educational media as a supplement to classroom instruction has been proven in many studies.

Continual advancement of content within the industrial and technological area requires greater utilization of educational media in the teacher training programs.

Student use of media is unlikely to occur unless *teachers* are trained to incorporate media into instructional programs.

A Final Note

One item of significance: the importance and acceptability of commercially available instructional materials have grown steadily and should be acknowledged. However, there still exists a greater need for students and teachers to develop instructional materials as part of the learning process at all levels of instruction.

References

Maley, Donald A. *"The Maryland Plan* and the behavioral task. analysis approach." Proceedings of the National Convention, Las Vegas: American Industrial Arts Association, 1969.

Scobey, Mary-Margaret. "Our Changing Technology: What's in It for Children," *Man/Society/Technology.* Vol. 32, No. 3, December, 1972. pp. 151-153.

AV CAN BE A TEACHER'S
BIGGEST HELP

Joe Kaiser

"The least likeable thing: it is automated ... less and less teacher and student relationships due to automated teaching ... "

The above statement was one parent's evaluation of an audiovisual course that his son had recently completed. The course, which covered small gasoline engines, was presented on a trial basis at a Midwest high school during the school year. This reaction, however, was the *only* negative parental comment among the dozens collected in a post-course "opinionaire." (A complete copy of the evaluation report can be obtained by writing Ken Cook Education Systems, 12855 W. Silver Spring Drive, P.O. Box 207, Butler, WI 53007.)

It was only one parent's opinion. But was it accurate? Not according to a comment from one of the participants: "The way the class runs, the teacher has time to work with every student in the class." The truth—that in an audiovisual course the teacher has more time for individual students—would seem to be directly opposite to the idea some people have of individually paced audiovisual programs.

Audiovisual programs provide help with the three functions of an industrial education teacher that consume the most time: (1) the transmittal of facts; (2) the demonstration of manual operations; (3) the inevitable repetition of (1) and (2). To the extent that the instructor is able to use audiovisual media for these tasks, he or she is freed for the main functions of a teacher: counseling, motivating and advising students individually.

Audiovisual in the 1940's

During the 1940's, when the author attended a trade high school, instructors had little time to build personal relationships with students. There was theory to be presented with blackboard and chalk. And there were skills to be demonstrated—over and over, as new students came along. We had only a few visual aids, such as wall charts, and an occasional movie or filmstrip shown to the class. Each of us was receiving information at a different rate, but it was all being transmitted at the same rate.

Then, as now, students varied in their individual achievements. Some took naturally to the subject being taught. They would have succeeded regardless of teaching media or methods because of talent and affinity for the field. Then there were a few who could not have advanced under any circumstances. They were completely devoid of any aptitude for the subject. Finally, there were those students in the middle. While they might have excelled, they often settled simply for "passing."

This middle group usually thinks that to ask the instructor to repeat or clarify a point or to ask for special help would be causing trouble. Also, they hate to admit in front of their peers that they are not "getting it." They become satisfied with less than the best when they should be claiming as their own all of the knowledge and skill the instructor can impart.

Audiovisual Today

Audiovisual media have come a long way in recent years. Improvements in film making and sound recording equipment coupled with new techniques like video tape, present today's instructor with opportunities for individualizing instruction to an extent undreamed of even a decade ago. The kind of relationship that used to exist between a master craftsman and his apprentice is now possible between the teacher and each student.

Audiovisual is an umbrella term that covers many diverse media. There is a bewildering array available today. For example, there are transparencies, slides, movies, filmstrips, film loops, reel and cassette audio and video tape, along with various combinations. Some media call for no action or response by the student. Some do call for a response. Some require easily-obtainable AV hardware while others require special projectors. Certain media can be edited or added to by the instructor. Others cannot. No longer is the question simply whether or not to incorporate audiovisual. Now the problem is to choose the right audiovisual program.

Most of the literature on audiovisual brings out the fact that each student can receive individual tutoring, that the material can be geared to fit the student's individual needs. What is often not mentioned is that instructors can and should make audiovisual fit their own needs. Only the individual instructor is in a position to prescribe what is to be taught, the manner in which it is to be presented, and what the student ought to know (or be able to do) as a result.

That is why the search for audiovisual software and hardware begins right in the classroom, laboratory or shop. Before consulting the school's audiovisual specialist or the suppliers' catalogs, the instructor must first do a good deal of homework.

How to Do It

The kind of thought processes that go into audiovisual planning can perhaps best be shown by an example. Assume that a male athletic director must teach a group of young women the game of baseball. They enter his class with no knowledge of the terms used or of the rules, and they know nothing of the playing skills.

After a few seasons in which he gives all training on the diamond, he begins to wonder if audiovisual might not help him produce a winning team in a shorter time. He reasons that if he did not have to spend so much time on the factual part of the game, he would have more time to help each player sharpen her playing skills.

The coach starts by breaking down his training into three parts. The first concern is knowledge: terminology, rules, etc. The second is skill: how to throw, field, bat, etc. The third is behavior: how each individual is to combine her knowledge and skills, and use them in concert with the others as a team. In a formal evaluation, he would call these the cognitive, psychomotor and affective domains.

Now the coach has two decisions to make: what subjects to cover with an audiovisual program and how to present them.

He might conclude that knowledge can best be imparted by means of a sound recording and a binder with illustrations and tests. Or he may feel that a film would be more effective. The film may contain staged demonstrations or clips from actual games to illustrate each point. He may desire student response to the audiovisual, or possibly may use the only test that really counts — on the field.

Then the coach turns his attention to skills. The student can become proficient in doing a task only by doing it, but the coach might conclude that certain fundamentals can be learned from visuals. For example, a bat should be swung in a certain plane, and a grounder should be fielded a certain way. If the young women could see these things demonstrated on film, some would pick up the skills right away. Others may need additional help. Still others may need to view the film and then practice the action, then view the film again and practice some more. Use of the visuals is strictly the choice of the individual.

In determining the ideal audiovisual program for him, the coach next turns his attention to hardware. He may want the hardware to be portable enough for the students to carry home. Perhaps it ought to be battery-operated for use outdoors. He probably would want the players to be able to operate it easily themselves.

Role of the AV Specialist

Finally, our hypothetical coach (or industrial education teacher) is ready to consult with an audiovisual specialist. It is only at this point that the special knowledge of audiovisual hardware and software can be used most advantageously. He describes his dream program. He lists what he wants the program to cover in order of importance. Hardware features are ranked according to desirability.

Now the AV specialist is in a position to provide specifications on the various types of available hardware and possible sources of software to fill his needs. It would be a mistake for an instructor to start looking for audiovisual before deciding on the message to be presented.

Importance of Planning

There is a second very important advantage in developing the message before choosing the medium. Your students will benefit from the planning! This process of planning for AV forces a review of everything in the existing program. Every item must justify itself. You will find students responding immediately to the improved organization and presentation of material.

Be open to the possibility that software suppliers may be able to improve on your program. But do not let that stop you from setting your own objectives first. As our old shop teacher used to put it, "If you don't know where you want to go, how will you know when you have arrived?"

PHOTO-TAPE UNITS PUT SAFETY FIRST   Ralph R. Bush

A constant dilemma for shop teachers is what to do about students who either check into class too late or are absent altogether when a safety lesson has been given on how to operate a particular machine. Do you ignore the rest of the class while you backtrack and re-explain for the benefit of one or two students, or do you ignore the few who missed the lesson, let them proceed on their own, and hope they won't make a serious mistake and get hurt?

Here's a solution that keeps the teacher from having to choose either of these poor alternatives. It can also be used to teach students who speak only foreign languages and therefore have trouble understanding lessons from teachers who are not bilingual. Since I am a woodworking teacher, I use the approach for lessons in this area, as the sample lesson shown here on operating the planer indicates, but the system can be applied to any subject matter.

Learning package. I use 18 standard safety lessons each year: 16 for the 16 different machines in my shop, one on general safety and shop deportment, and one on the seven steps for squaring a board to desired dimensions using the heavy machines. For each of these lessons, I have made up a three-ring loose-leaf notebook containing a step-by-step picture presentation of all the aspects of the lesson. Along with the notebook of displayed photos goes an instant-loading audio tape cartridge cassette which explains the pictures while the student is looking at them. Each of the cassettes is kept with the notebook it explains, so that, if a student needs the instructions for a particular lesson, I just pull the notebook, snap the cassette into the player, and in less than 30 seconds, the student has an individual learning package completely set up for him.

Among the most obvious advantages of this approach are the amount of trouble it eliminates and the time it saves. There is no projector or screen to set up and no room to darken, so that the student can catch up on the missed lesson immediately and without keeping the rest of the class from making use of the other facilities in the shop.

Here in southern California, however, where many students speak Spanish either predominantly or exclusively, the notebook-cassette system is also important as a means for solving the language barrier problem. I asked the school's foreign language department to translate my cassettes into Spanish. Now each of my notebooks is accompanied by two cassettes—one in English, the other in Spanish. Although I speak no Spanish myself, my Spanish-speaking students learn as fast as any.

Plan ahead. Clear pictures and a good lesson take quite a bit of prior planning, but the advance preparation will show in the quality of the finished product—and in how easily the lesson is understood by the students using it. First, make up a list of all the items you want to photograph for the lesson; then take all the time you need setting up the pictures. Look through the view-finder and study

Reprinted by permission of the author and *School Shop* 35 (March 1976):35-37.

the shot carefully, making certain that from the angle you have selected you will be showing what you really need to show. Consider the shot from alternative angles, and then choose the best one.

Pose the people in your photos in natural working positions, checking first to see that they are wearing eye protection and appropriate clothing and that no safety rules are being broken in the action to be photographed unless, of course, you want to draw the student's attention specifically to what he should *not* be doing.

Examine the background that will appear in the photo as you plan to take it, and remove anything that will clutter the picture or tend to distract the viewer from the step you are trying to illustrate. To point out a specific part of a machine or a specific setting, a large arrow and an "X" can be made out of heavy construction paper and then applied to the location in question with double-backed tape before the photograph is taken; this leaves no question in the mind of the viewer about what you are referring to in the corresponding recorded explanation.

Available light. Photos may be shot using a 35mm camera mounted on a tripod with Tri-X film which has a standard ASA speed of 400. A film speed of 1/125 sec. and a stop of f2 usually is effective; these settings allow using the overhead fluorescent lights in the room. I used flash on my earliest shots but gave it up when I discovered that the flash was reflecting off the machined surfaces, causing "hot spots" on the film. Using the available light can work much better, but be sure to use a tripod, since the indicated shutter speed is rather slow.

Determine beforehand that all photographs for a given lesson will be shot either vertically or horizontally. It may seem easier at the time the individual photos are being taken to mix vertical and horizontal shots, but doing this will make the sequence of photos difficult to display as a whole unit.

Finding an effective way to display the photo sequence may pose a problem anyway. The best arrangement I have found is using vinyl double-view sheet protectors available from most photo supply stores. These make clear pages for placing photos back to back, and they fit standard three- or five-ring notebooks. The ones I use are made to hold eight 3½ by 5 in. prints.

Script writing. When the photography is finished and it is time to make the cassettes, lay out the pictures in their proper order and write a script to accompany them. Double check what you've written to make sure everything essential to the lesson has been covered. Sometimes it can be helpful to record the tape while you are situated at the machine to be explained in the lesson, perhaps even having it turned on for added emphasis. When you've finished making the recording, play it back and check it against your pictures and script. If everything has been explained as you wanted it to be and you find it up to your standards, punch out the two small perforated tabs on the back of the cassette; this will prevent the tape from being accidentally erased or recorded over.

One of the major features of this picture-tape type of lesson presentation is that more details can be explained to the student in far less time than it would take to go through the same operations on the actual shop machine. But keep in mind that this method should be used as a means of getting around a problem; it is still no substitute for a good teacher.

VI

PRODUCTION OF MATERIALS IN THE
MEDIA CENTER AND CLASSROOM

More and more teachers and media specialists are beginning to provide students with the opportunity to become involved in the production of materials that they will find useful in their classrooms. As a result of such activity, students find themselves as active participants in their own learning. They are motivated to interact with their peers, to read or research a topic before consuming materials, to learn the techniques of storyboarding and scripting, and to produce a product that can be shared with others.

All of the articles in this section demonstrate how nonprint production can serve as a motivator for active student participation. Carlene Mello Aborn in "Multi-Image Productions Are Magical Motivators" describes the sequence of events that provided her junior high students with the opportunity to put together a multi-image production. The arrangement of the minicourse that Ms. Aborn designed is clearly explained so that the reader could easily replicate the project. Another group of junior high school students' activity with a videotape system is examined in the article by Linda Kahn. The author not only describes the variety of uses that her class found for the VTR but also how others within her school utilized the medium. Douglas K. Meyer in "The Photographic Essay in Geographic Instruction" gives a detailed account of the steps to be taken in organizing an essay using photographs. The procedures for planning and executing a photo essay are explained along with a discussion of some basic principles of photo composition. The concluding article in this section, "The Case for Filmstrips: Producing Filmstrips in the Classroom" by Doris P. Miller, begins by posing questions to the reader on the true value of filmmaking in the English classroom. The author then proceeds to explain why she felt, after an initial encounter with such a production, that "there can be few better ways to teach reading, writing, and oral expression on the secondary level than working with students in producing sound filmstrips and slide-sound productions."

MULTI-IMAGE PRODUCTIONS ARE
MAGICAL MOTIVATORS

Carlene Mello Aborn

It was Saturday, March 8, 1975, the second day of an institute on "Principals and Librarians: Team for Curricular Change," which was jointly sponsored by National Association of Secondary School Principals and the American Association of School Librarians. Our presentation, "Azalea Middle School's Media Program; Its Relationship to Curricular Change," had been given on the previous day and now, my principal and I were to view a program from Santa Fe Community College in Gainesville, Florida.

After the houselights had dimmed, our eyes were drawn to the visual images that were bursting forth in beautiful rhythmic patterns on three large screens. The haunting melody of the song "Vincent" began playing while, in fascination, I watched slides of Van Gogh's masterpieces projected in single concept, in double images, or in magnificent panoramas across the three screens. I became so immersed in this vital new experience, I felt it ended much too soon. There was a stillness in the room as the program came to a close, but finally the silence was broken by unabashed applause followed by excited chattering.

I glanced at my principal, Scotty East, who was seated beside me, hoping to see reflected in his expression the same wondrous feeling I was enjoying, and at the same time I was thinking about how we could use this type of program to motivate and teach our middle school students. This would never become reality if Mr. East didn't buy into the idea. But after one look at him, I knew our kids were on their way. His expression was that of disbelief and amazement. He finally looked at me and said, "That was really something else. What an exhilarating experience! If it made this kind of an impression on us, just think how our students would react. We have to find out how it's done and whether or not it's feasible for middle school kids." And so began the exciting, challenging venture into the realm of the magic of multi-image.

When some of the crowd had dissipated, we approached Ron Slawson, who presented the multimedia program. He informed us that the program we had seen had been produced by his students as a requirement for a multi-media production course. Mr. Slawson's obvious enthusiasm for this media was contagious as he explained the basic concepts involved in multi-image production. As he talked and answered our questions, I took notes feverishly. I even drew a diagram of the equipment set-up so that on Monday morning I would have some base from which to proceed. Because of the complexity of this type of presentation, I knew that I would have to become knowledgeable about the various aspects of this concept, if I was to attempt a similar program with our students. We continued to pick Ron Slawson's brain for some time, and I'm certain he breathed a long sigh of relief when we finally let him go.

Reprinted by permission of the author and R. R. Bowker Company/A Xerox Corporation from *School Library Journal* 23 (April 1977):33-37.

On Monday morning as soon as I arrived at work, I checked on all the available equipment that was suited to multi-image programs. To my delight, I found that we had four Kodak carousel projectors with zoom lenses and remote control buttons, a Canon 35mm camera, two Kodak Ektagraphic Visualmakers, many reel type monaural tape recorders, and a number of medium-sized screens. Although we did not have the other required pieces of equipment; Wollensak Dissolve Unit; Wollensak Digi-Cue or a Wollensak 2551 Cassette tape recorder, I felt that our learning center had enough equipment with which to start.

As part of my self-training program, I began to experiment, with three carousel projectors, each containing a tray of assorted slides. I taped each projector's remote control button, sequentially from left to right, on a small board. Because of the small size of our learning center, I painted a wall white and used it in place of the three screens. To create a mood, I played a variety of taped instrumental background music. By depressing the remote control button in different sequences, I found I could literally tell a story or convey a feeling visually. Even at this primitive level of operation, it was easy to see the strong potential of this media as a motivating tool or teaching device.

Because the learning center adjoins the media center, the activities taking place were in view of the many students using the center and it was not long before the music and the images on the wall drew the students in to watch and ask questions. Needless to say, they were eager to try their hand at this new activity. They were really turned on. Watching their reactions as they experimented with various combinations of visual concepts, I began to formulate plans for a course in media production, to commence in September, 1975.

Our school schedule includes a 45 minute block of time at the end of each day. This period, called Special Interest, enables students to take a variety of nonacademic mini-courses throughout the school year. Ordinarily, I do not teach a Special Interest mini-course because the media center is kept open during this last period for business as usual. I realized that if I undertook this multi-image project, it would mean additional work for my staff. So, before proceeding further, I discussed the possibility of teaching a mini-course in media production. My staff, which includes two paraprofessionals, a library clerk, and an audio-visual aide, agreed that I should try it, and one of my paraprofessionals, Becky Johnson, volunteered to assist.

My next step was to secure permission and financial support from my principal. The very nature of media production meant that we would have to have adequate funding for film, magicubes, film processing, slide trays, and tapes. I also anticipated the purchase of a dissolve unit sometime in the near future. Our media center budget, already strained, could not support this activity.

I asked for funding and received a pleasant surprise. It was fortunate that Mr. East had been exposed to multi-image because when I approached him with my plan to teach a mini-course in media production with a strong emphasis on multi-image, he enthusiastically gave his approval, assuring me that money from the school's general fund would be made available for whatever needs our course objectives required. The next step was to write a Special Interest mini-course description and objectives and submit it to our Special Interest Coordinator. My multimedia production course description and objectives read as follows:

This course is designed to present instruction so that each participant will develop the necessary skills to prepare a multi-media production. Special emphasis will be placed on developing an appreciation for the functional and aesthetic value of multi-media.

Emphasis will be placed on the importance of planning in step-by-step procedures from all ideas to their effective implementation through a hands-on approach. Participants will be instructed in the operation of the various equipment necessary to multimedia technique.

Objectives

• Knowledge of the media and equipment necessary for multimedia production.

• Ability to use a storyboard as a planning device.

• Ability to design a media production.

• Ability to evaluate a variety of media production using established criteria.

• Skill in selecting appropriate themes for media productions.

With most of these essential details behind me, and approval having been granted to teach a Multi-media Course, I was able to continue my efforts at becoming more knowledgeable about this concept. And, by the time the school year ended, I was beginning to feel qualified to teach multi-image production.

First Steps

Although school opened in late August, Special Interest classes did not begin until the middle of September. In the interim, I made preparations for my students. I requested that the school purchase a Wollensak 3M AV32 Dissolve Unit, a Wollensak 3M Pro 6 Digi-Cue, and a Wollensak 2551 Cassette tape recorder. I also stressed our great need for a large light table as slide sorters would not be adequate for setting up a multi-image program. Once again our principal came through, and we were able to order the necessary items. Much to my surprise and delight, our plant maintenance staff made a functional light table from discarded items which included an intercom desk unit, four 47 inch Fluorescent lamps, a power switch, power cord, and one sheet of frosted plexiglass. The total cost was less than *twenty dollars.*

In planning for my group of students, I decided that it might be a good idea to start a slide collection. This would help to keep our expenses down, and also give us a foundation on which to build. All staff members having duplicate slides or discards were requested to donate them to us. This request also went to our parent's organization. The response was excellent. As the slides came in, we categorized them into general subject areas such as U.S.; Science; Children; Winter; Flowers, etc. They were then stored in single compartmented slide holders in three-ring notebooks. Using this method, students could remove the slide holder and view twenty slides on the light table, rather than pull out many individual slides. This method proved to be both a time saver and a slide saver.

Finally, the day of our first multimedia production class arrived. The class enrollment was limited to 18 students because it was felt that this would be the maximum number my assistant and I could handle to accomplish our objectives and provide optimum assistance to each student. As the class gathered, it was immediately apparent that the group was extremely diverse. All three grade levels, sixth through eighth, were represented. There was almost an equal number of boys and girls and their scholastic abilities covered a wide range. We also acquired a couple of students with behavior problems—a truly heterogeneous group. As I took the roll and observed each one, I couldn't help but wonder whether or not these students would be able to cope with the complexities of this mini-course.

Banishing these questions, for which I had no immediate answers, from my mind, I briefly described what our nine-week session would involve and explained what would be expected of each of them. They were informed that the school would supply all the necessary materials for their presentations, and that, in turn, the programs would become the property of the school. Those students desiring to keep their productions would have to furnish their own materials.

A brief handout indicating and explaining the various multimedia options available in this course was handed out. The list included Super 8/sound, transparency/sound, filmstrip/sound, slide-sound, and multi-image/sound. Each student was asked to take the handout home, study it carefully, talk it over with his or her parents, and select one of the formats within the next two days. By Wednesday, the students had made their selections. Three chose Super 8/sound; four selected transparency/sound; two decided on filmstrip/sound; three chose slide/sound; and multi-image was the choice of six. Eight compatible groups of two or three members each were organized.

The remainder of the first week was spent in developing class rules and general procedures to be followed in producing any multimedia program. We discussed theme selection, emphasizing several important points: (1) The purpose for the program must be determined. (2) Some themes are more easily visualized than others. (3) Availability of slides or pictures from which a visual could be made must be considered. (4) The audience for which the program is being produced must be taken into account. After this discussion, the students were asked to bring in a list of possible themes to share at the next class meeting. They returned with lists of theme possibilities that were nearly as diverse as our group.

During the next two days, all of their themes were evaluated using the criteria we had established previously. Finally, each group had reached an agreement on a general theme. At this point, Ms. Johnson took over the responsibility for those working in Super 8, transparency, and filmstrips. I directed those groups working in slide-sound and multi-image.

As the main thrust of the mini-course was to introduce multi-image presentations to our school, I really concentrated in this particular area, assisting and encouraging my students to extend themselves further than ever before because they were a pioneer group. I wanted them to achieve success and a feeling of accomplishment.

In addition to those doing slide-sound, my section included two eighth-grade girls who chose to visualize *Winter Wonderland*, two eighth-grade boys selected *Born Free*, two boys (sixth and seventh graders) decided on *My Country*, and an eighth-grade boy, who wanted to work alone on *Feelings*. With the number of groups I had and the short time allocated, it was paramount that everyone was well organized and working to capacity every moment.

Production

Once all the themes and accompanying sound tracks were selected, the next step was teaching the students to plot programs on storyboards. Instead of making up a storyboard, we used a form that was developed by The 3M Company. The value of a storyboard as a preliminary step in multi-image production cannot be overstressed. Sketches or word descriptions can be used in developing the visual sequences. I found that students who are not artists often get turned off if they feel they must do sketches.

In the audio section of the storyboard, one member of the group wrote the words to the song they were visualizing. Generally speaking, one space per song phrase was used. Next, each group had to decide on what visuals they were going to use for each phrase. These decisions, made early in the process, changed many times, because frequently students could not find the visual they wanted. When they did decide on what kinds of slides they needed, they went through the slide files. When this was accomplished, the next time-consuming and often frustrating job was to locate suitable pictures from which they could make slides using the Visualmaker. This was the stage during which the less capable, less motivated students often experienced difficulty. Looking through picture files, magazines, calendars, and books for just the *right* picture, took a lot of patience and perseverance. Almost daily, students had to be encouraged to search further and not settle on the first if it wasn't good enough.

Because of the almost foolproof design in using the Visualmaker, every student acquired skill at it and before long, we did not have to supervise anyone. Through experience with the Visualmaker we found tht it was useless to crop a picture before it was taken, because the black construction paper, normally used as a framing device, shows up on the slide with a grayish cast. The students were taught to crop after the slides were processed, using photographic tape. There are numerous brands of tape that may be used for this purpose — the choice of tape seems to be a matter of personal preference and comparative cost. What is important in this process, is that each student acquires the ability to crop with straight lines. Geometric shapes, often used for special effect slides, can be formed through the use of cropping tape. Each group worked diligently. They found that some of the best sources for pictures were old calendars, magazines, and pictorial books in series.

Each day, one student was instructed in the use of the equipment and its setup. The student was given a diagram of the equipment hookup and with this information and a demonstration, it did not take long before this technique had been mastered by all involved. In addition to learning the procedures for setting up equipment, students were taught to change projection lamps, clean tape recorder heads, and to make a cassette tape copy from a recording using an audio cable, instead of a microphone.

One of the tasks most enjoyed by the students was that of creating title and credit slides. We used different techniques. A few used rub-on letters over a picture; others used plastic letters laid upon a picture; some wrote in script across decorative shelf paper, and still others wrote their titles in the sand and photographed that.

In reading about multi-image in the *Journal of the Association for Multi-Image*, I discovered a source of plastic opaque slides which I promptly obtained. I found that they were much more satisfactory than the black slides and poster board squares we had used in the past.

By the end of the fifth week, all of the new equipment had arrived and now we were really in business. The *Winter Wonderland* group was ready to lay out their program on the light table to time it and evaluate the composition of their slide sequences. While playing their sound track, they simulated the sequences as they would appear on the screen. Timing each sequence was critical — the visuals had to be coordinated with the audio.

In directing these students in multi-media production, I used a booklet published by 3M entitled "How to Prepare a Multi-Media Storyboard." It was most beneficial; however, the technique suggested for cueing was too difficult for my students to comprehend. So I developed my own, less complicated system.

The *Winter Wonderland* group, having successfully timed their program, was now ready to insert their slides in the four trays, having first labeled each tray according to its position in the projector placement. Each slide was also identified in a manner that would enable anyone to replace the slide in its correct position should its removal be necessary.

The next step was to view each tray of slides individually making sure that each slide was in its correct position; right-side-up, etc. Once this was done, it was time to rehearse with the Digi-Cue and sound track, using the storyboard as a script. Seeing the first of the programs near completion was fantastic shot-in-the-arm for the other groups. The whole course was revitalized as each group wanted to see their own productions shown on the screens.

The *Winter Wonderland* group then proceeded to program their presentation. They had rehearsed many times and were anxious to have it completely finished. Once they realized that should they make an error in cueing, it could be easily erased without harming the sound track, they were much more at ease and managed to get their presentation cued in one try. Now they were able to relax, sit back and enjoy the product of the many long weeks of work. The members of the group shared a real feeling of accomplishment — they were full of pride and were walking on "Cloud 9." They showed their program at every opportunity.

All the other groups finished their programs although some of them had to spend some extra time after school so that they could finish by the end of the nine-week session.

We now had completed four multi-image programs to share with the rest of the school. Practically everyone was aware that we were doing exciting things in multimedia production. We had had numerous requests to share the students' productions with the faculty and student body, and so we began scheduling teams into the media center for the purpose of viewing these programs. Because of the size of the center, the screens we had were too small, and we had to use two king-sized bed sheets hung from the ceiling in place of the screens. The students were so adept at setting the equipment up that they could have everything ready to go in ten minutes, including moving all the tables to allow for a larger seating capacity.

After the first showing to which the audience response was overwhelmingly positive, the school's Assistant Principal, Bill Beyer, put his hand on my shoulder and said, "You have just opened up Pandora's Box. Now every kid in the building will want to do a multi-image production."

Far-reaching Results

Fortunately or unfortunately, depending on how you look at life and work, he was right. Requests came in from teachers and students, asking that we present our programs as a kick-off activity for inter-disciplinary units, as a means of motivating students. We tried to honor all the requests, as enthusiasm for multimedia and multi-image was at an all-time high.

Soon, multi-image production was incorporated into curriculum activities. No longer did I teach it as a Special Interest, as we had so many productions as an outgrowth of classroom activities that I needed the Special Interest period to work with students already involved in multi-image. I was busier with media than at any other time in my professional career — and I was loving every second of it.

We showed our students' productions at a Back-to-School night in the spring. Disbelief was written all over the parents' faces. They almost refused to believe that middle school students could do anything that seemed so complicated and have it turn out so beautifully.

Students from the University of South Florida often visited our school and they, too, were flabbergasted that middle school students could design multi-image productions.

We entered three of our best multi-image productions in the 1976 Pinellas County Media Festival. *My Country* took first place, *Born Free* won second place, and *Feelings* took third. You can imagine the pride of these students at their outstanding success in a production format that up to this point, had been the almost exclusive domain of junior colleges, universities, and industry.

Near the end of the first year of multi-media production the students had produced twenty multi-image programs, twenty-five slide-sound presentations, and numerous other multimedia programs.

Two of our students who had started on multi-image productions late in the year, did not have an opportunity to finish. They knew that I would be at school during the summer, so these two dedicated girls, Mary Liberty and Sheri Waldeck, spent most of their vacation time finishing their projects. Sheri's production was our first truly instructional multi-image. Her subject was *Glaciers* and she worte her own script, selected her pictures and background music, and coordinated the whole project beautifully. Mary's topic was *Music of the Union*, a very moving visualization of the Civil War era. When two active girls are willing to sacrifice much of their vacation, I think it is safe to say that they were really turned on by multi-image. Keep in mind that they were eighth graders, not returning to this school this year and there was no scholastic record or grade involved.

This year, in October, at the Florida League of Middle School's Conference, a group of last year's students and I presented a program based on our students' multi-image productions. I know our program made an impression, judging from the many positive and information-seeking letters I've received.

At the November 1976 meeting of the National Middle School's Association Convention, held in St. Louis, Missouri, I once again presented our program — this time to a group of administrators. Their response was overwhelmingly positive. One member of the group approached me after the presentation and said, "I was on my way to another meeting, your door was open, I heard the music, saw the beautiful visuals on the screens and I was captivated. I never did make it to the other meeting. This has been the highlight of the conference."

In January, Linda Hobelmann, a parent volunteer who was turned on by multi-image and now donates all of her extra time to helping us with our media program, assisted me in conducting a workshop in Ft. Walton Beach, Florida for the Florida Right to Read Program, and we were invited to bring our programs to Ft. Lauderdale this spring.

Summary

Presently, at Azalea Middle School, we have amassed nearly 2500 slides for students' use. We have six multi-image programs in various stages of production, including topics such as *The History of St. Petersburg, Florida, The Sand and the Sea*, and *Fantastic Voyage.*

"Have program, will travel" has become our slogan as we strive to introduce the magic motivator—multi-image—to teachers and administrators who we hope will encourage and enable their students to become involved with multi-image production.

Multi-image programs are now being used with great success throughout the county as a means of presenting an overview of the various segments of our educational system to school boards. In this day of tightening budgets and accountability, programs that accent the positive aspects of education in a meaningful and yet aesthetic manner are of great and lasting value.

References

Atherton, Lawrence L. "A Comparison of Movie and Multiple Image Presentation Techniques on Affective and Cognitive Learning." Unpublished Ph.D. dissertation, Michigan State University, 1971.

Beckman, Carl. "The Multi-Image Roadshow Blues." *Journal of the Association for Multi-Images* (Winter, 1976) p. 4.

Bollman, Charles G. " The Effect of Large-Screen, Multi-Image Display on Evaluative Meaning." Unpublished Ph.D. dissertation, Michigan State University, 1970.

Burke, Ken. "Multi-Image Used in Workshop." *Journal of the Association for Multi-Images* (Winter, 1977) p. 5.

Ingli, Donald. "Teaching a Basic AV Course by the Multi-Image Technique." Southern Illinois University, ERIC document ED 060634, April 1972.

Maguire, James. "Who's Got Multi-Image? And What Are They Doing With It." *Audiovisual Instructon.* January, 1977. p. 54.

Slawson, Ron. "How to Prepare a Multi-Media Presentation." *Journal of the Association for Multi-Images*, (Winter, 1977) p. 12.

(The Association for Multi-Image is at 947 Old York Rd., Abington, Pa. 19001.)

Basic Production Equipment

Audio cable
Audio mixer
Camera (35mm)

Carousel projectors (4 with zoom lens)
Cassette tape recorder (Wollensak model 2551 or 2570)
Digi-cue (3M)
Dissolve unit (3M AV 32 or AV 33)
Ektagraphic Visualmaker (Kodak)
Light table or slide porters
Reel to reel tape recorder
Cartridge film (126, Kodachrome 64)
Cassette Tapes
Magi cubes
Opaque slides and tape
Slide masks (Optional)
Slide trays (4 drums for each program)

Sources for Materials

Eastman Kodak Company, Rochester, N.Y. 14650. (carousel projectors, slide trays, lenses, etc.)

Kaiser Products Corporation, Photo and AV Equipment Division, 3555 N. Prospect St., Colorado Springs, Colo. 80907. (opaque slides, slide masks, plastic mounts, etc.)

3M Company, Visual Products Division, 3M Center, St. Paul, Minn. 55101. (dissolvers, digi-cues, cassette recorders, etc.)

20th Century Plastics, Inc., 3628 Crenshaw Blvd., Los Angeles, Calif. 90016. (vinyl slide pages)

VTR IN THE CLASSROOM – OR –
HOW I LEARNED TO STOP WORRYING
AND START SAVING CARDBOARD BOXES   Linda Kahn

Last week in my classroom, New York City was once again demolished by King Kong. Clutched in his right hand was his terrified victim (his sister's toy doll); his left hand concealed a deadly and powerful weapon (a chalk eraser). Behind him were the skyscrapers of the city (drawn on the blackboard by the production crew).

Kong reached for new heights as he climbed the stepladder at the base of the skyline. With a threatening roar and a mighty sweep of his arm, he erased New York. Then the bell rang, King Kong slipped out of his Halloween gorilla costume, and joined the director, the floor manager, the camera person, and the rest of the students on their way to Science, Math, Music, and French. New York was a shambles. So was my classroom.

Our's is not a sophisticated set-up. Twenty-five heterogeneous seventh graders meet daily for forty minutes. Access to a video recorder and monitor is limited to one week each month. Much of the materials we use are homemade. But despite these limitations – maybe because of them – the students are developing abilities and perceptions for a critical contemporary medium, and learning basic language arts skills in the process.

It would be easy to duplicate our efforts elsewhere. All it takes is a spirit of adventure, a sense of enjoyment, and a willingness to grow. So if you don't mind building props from discarded refrigerator cartons or videotaping a documentary in the nurse's office, if you can make extension cords appear magically and aren't perplexed when a fuse blows, and if you think all this might be fun – then you, too, can help students improve their reading, writing, and thinking while developing their awareness of the TV medium.

One of the things we've learned is that video is a powerful tool that can put people who make decisions directly in touch with those whom these decisions will affect. For example, members of my class produced a documentary in which students, teachers, parents, and the principal discussed student proposals for energy conservation. Titled "The Energy Crisis OR When You're Hot You're Hot and When You're Not ... ," the program was shown at a School Committee meeting and is now available at the public library.

Parents are working with students to produce "Why Can't a Girl Have a Goal?" They want to see a girls' hockey league sponsored by the public schools. Their concern is real: currently it may cost a girl $500.00 for her equipment and ice time. Although we have a girl goalie on the boys' team, the parents are interested in an all-girl league. So they and the students are making a tape which they plan to take to School Committees in the Boston area – thus using the media to inform, to communicate, to change.

Originally printed in *Media and Methods* 11 (April 1975):40-41. Used with permission.

A folklore class is using the media to preserve the oral traditions of Watertown. On the order of *Foxfire*, they are collecting local tales, songs, dances, recipes, and superstitions. Plans include a videotaped series on the city, as well as a magazine complete with student-made photographs.

The biggest problems we face are time and availability of equipment. The one week per month when we can use the videotape recorder and monitor is spent entirely on production. We begin storyboarding, script writing, and graphics and props production ten days in advance. To facilitate planning and rehearsing, I have made cameras out of cardboard boxes, using cut-down paper towel rollers for lenses. The crews practice with these "cameras" to get a feel for production. Time is also saved by using slides to demonstrate the operation of equipment. When the VTR does arrive, it is a familiar tool. A minimum amount of time is spent reviewing its operation.

I begin the course by explaining mass media and by describing all the equipment we will use. Since students will be using these tools, they must demonstrate their ability to handle them. This includes identifying the parts and functions of the video camera: f-stop, zoom, focus, trigger, tally light, eyepiece/monitor. The camera movements and shots are also practiced. Since we rotate crew responsibilities, each student learns how the director, floor manager, camera person, audio person, talent and graphics person function during a production. After passing a test, students go around the school in pairs to practice using the Portapak. (One pair accidentally taped someone cheating during a French test.)

Early assignments involve studying camera shots by using comic strips. With cartoon examples of close-ups, long shots, etc., students discuss the appropriateness and effectiveness of the different camera angles. (I've been asked to "pan right" or "dolly out" because someone couldn't see the blackboard.)

Another preliminary assignment involves designing a storyboard to describe a process: for example, how to make a peanut butter and jelly sandwich. These storyboards have a frame for each shot, a column for audio instruction, and a column for the video description of the shot. We first discuss expository writing—this *is* an English class, remember—then students write paragraphs which they translate into visual shots. The focus is on clear, accurate directions. (An honor student surprised everyone with her storyboard of "How to Cheat on a Test.")

Selecting a simple script, I divide the class into four or five crews. Each produces the same "how-to" show, preparing new graphics, threading the VTR, constructing the set. Repeating the same production puts everyone at ease. A class evaluation follows each video effort. We discuss the crew's objectives, their planning, the camera point of view, lighting, and sound. Additionally, the crew evaluates its effectiveness as a group.

More complex productions include the use of "special effects." Sheet metal thunder and flashing overhead lights create storms. Squeaking desk tops simulate bats. The victim unknowingly drinks poison and the room spins (the camera person spins the camera), her vision is blurred (the camera is out of focus). Or, the scene is a wrestling match and one fighter has just been knocked out (fade to black), he's up, he's down again (zoom in and zoom out for emphasis). A dissolve effect may be created by ending a shot out of focus, then changing the scene before coming back in focus. Sound effects records, music, and audio dubbing matched with graphics and live action are simple tools that can be successfully used even in early efforts.

Sets consist of simple devices, often just decorated cardboard boxes. One crew advertised waterbeds which were nothing more than cardboard frames and water balloons. A videotape may be shot using only graphics. One of our most successful tapes was based on Shirley Jackson's "The Lottery." While one boy operated the camera, a second pulled the colored construction paper graphics, and several others provided the dialogue, music, and sound effects. Their second production was an adaptation of "Richard Cory," but, instead of framing the graphics, the camera person (feeling the glow of success) shot the scenes, the stand, and his friend pulling the graphics. We decided that it was intentional, and they now had a demonstration tape of their process.

A highlight of the course is the class' use of the black-and-white studio at Boston University's School of Education. (If we had two cameras, a special effects generator, and a mini-studio set-up, the trip would not be necessary — and we'd miss it.) Hiding behind cardboard racing cars, telephone booths, bags of costumes and make-up, the students take public transportation into Boston. Once there, I divide them into three or four crews of seven students. While Crew One produces the show, Crew Two watches — director observes director, etc. Crew Three provides the talent. Then we rotate the crews and begin the procedure again. Parodies of *The Wizard of Oz* were excellent starting points since extra people could double as Munchkins. With the swirl of the curtain and people yelling "Whoooosh," the tornado hits Kansas City as well as the studio.

The most crucial element contributing to the success of this course is the continual feedback and encouragement that the students receive from me, and from each other. The end result has been that now, after many dilemmas and disappointments, successes and surprises, the students are comfortable, productive, and learning. Or at least they were yesterday.

THE PHOTOGRAPHIC ESSAY IN
GEOGRAPHIC INSTRUCTION

Douglas K. Meyer

A number of recent articles reflect the increased awareness and the improved utilization of flat pictures and slides as effective instructional media tools in geographic education.[1] But the photographic essay as an instructional technique used by either teachers or students has not been discussed in the geographic literature. Many geographers shoot hundreds or even thousands of slides in their travels as they seek to understand man's occupance of this spaceship earth. All too often many of the slides that are shown in classroom teaching situations portray a lack of understanding of proper light exposure, depth of field and the principles of photo composition. Moreover, the slide presentation frequently suggests no rationale for the organization.

This paper will focus on outlining and briefly commenting on the procedures for planning and executing a photographic essay. Owing to the importance of photo composition, special attention will be given to some of the basic rules and principles.

Being a universal language, photography today exists as an effective form of communication.[2] Pictures that are pleasing have impact; in other words, they serve to emphasize a single idea. [3] Consequently pictures can provide an answer to a problem or question, thus, aiding the teacher in making an idea more relevant to students. Photography in teaching should aim towards allowing the pictures to tell the story. Likewise, a true photo essay would normally not need narration. Since good photos are made, careful pre-planning of the photographic essay will probably determine much of the overall final quality.

The particular outline offered in Figure 1 should be helpful to both teachers and students in planning and executing a color slide photo essay. Depending on the educational and experience level, students could work either in teams or as individuals.

Comments on the Outline

Probably the most important step in preparing a photo essay using color slides, as in any good learning situation, is to analyze carefully the total idea (Fig. 1). If the pre-planning does not include an analysis of the objective, audience and subject matter, the fundamental goal of providing the learner with a visualized experience which he can understand will not be achieved. Tailoring the pictures to the experience level of the audience will help to guarantee the communicating of the story or main idea.

Reprinted by permission of the author and *Journal of Geography* 72 (September 1973):11-26, National Council for Geographic Education.

Figure 1

PLANNING AND EXECUTING A PHOTOGRAPHIC ESSAY

1. Analyze the Total Idea
   A. Determine the *objective* or *basic concept*
   B. Determine the *audience*
   C. Determine the *subject matter*
   D. Determine the relationship between the objective, audience and subject matter
   E. Determine the form that will best convey the subject matter or the central idea

2. Break Idea into Shots
   A. Determine each shot
   B. Determine narration, music, etc. for each individual shot

3. Analyze Each Shot
   A. As an individual picture
   B. As it relates to the overall objective
   C. As it relates to the preceding shot and the following shot

4. Choose Settings for Shots
   A. analyze the relationship of the setting to the shot objective
   B. Analyze the relationship of the setting to the sequence objective
   C. Analyze the setting in terms of the audience and subject matter

5. Decide upon Treatment
   A. Determine if it is to be dramatic, humorous, educational, documentary
   B. Determine additional factors such as sound (narration or music) captions, descriptions

6. Determine Technical Factors
   A. Type of camera, film, lights, etc.
   B. Form of final project

7. Prepare Treatment
   A. Determine content of each shot
   B. Sketch each shot on cards or scrip sheet
   C. Rough out narration or music
   D. Sequence shots
   E. Try out

8. Shoot Film
   A. Set shutter speed
   B. Set aperture opening
   C. Focus camera
   D. Expose film

9. Photo Essay Compilation
   A. Sequence shots as per story board
   B . Write final script
   C. Rehearse
   D. Present

Source: Based on notes from a graduate course, *Photography in Instruction*, taught by Dr. Robert Kline, Michigan State University, Winter Quarter, 1968.

Next break the idea into shots, then, analyze each shot as an individual picture, as it relates to the overall objective and to the preceding shot and the following shot (Fig. 1). After choosing the settings for the shots, analyze the relationship of the setting to the shot objective and to the sequence objective. The foregoing ideas are essential, if the pictures are to relate the story. One way this can be accomplished is by using a series of slides to lead people, for example, distant shot, medium shot and close-up shot. Besides, by varying the length of time the slide remains on the screen, changing viewpoints and settings the viewer is kept guessing. Filling the gaps and providing transition links can be achieved by using maps and by taking pictures of art and mueseum displays. Keeping the picture simple, however, is the key to success. Such a good photograph should clarify, emphasize and dramatize for the viewer a single point concerning the subject matter.[4]

By nature students differ in their perception of life and day to day events. As a consequence, some students tend to verbalize and visualize their ideas, more or less, in either a dramatic, a humorous or a documentary framework. Deciding upon the treatment, then, enables the students to provide a very creative touch to their project (Fig. 1). At this point in the planning stage of the photo essay, the need for such additional factors as sound (narration or music), captions and descriptions should be determined.

Previous picture taking experience, cameras available (instamatics to single-lens reflex) and amount of money for expenses will probably specify the level of technical factors incorporated into the project. If the teacher and students have little background in photography, he can capitalize on the situation by having a parent who is a good amateur photographer, or a professional photographer talk to the class. However, at the high school level, student class reports on the mechanics and basic principles of photographic composition could be utilized as a self-learning experience. Showing an example of a photo essay would also help to create interest and establish a level of quality. Because a photographic essay project requires a variety of tasks for completion, each student of a team should find his niche where his talents will contribute to the success of the project. Of course at the college level, one individual will probably perform all aspects of the photographic essay.

Critical to the success of any photo essay is preparing the treatment prior to any actual shooting of the pictures. Since an analysis of the content of each shot has already been made, prepare a script card for each slide (Fig. 2). Such a script card as in Figure 2 can be easily duplicated in the quantities needed. Each script card should include: (1) rough sketch of the proposed slide, (2) slide number, (3) slide title, (4) audio or narration for slide if needed and (5) technical information for the photographer. Keep the pictures simple and not busy. Varying the types of slides is a necessity for holding the viewer's interest. Sometimes a cartoon or a single word slide might convey an idea best. Similarly, examine each picture in its relationship to the overall objective, the preceding shot and following shot. After

Figure 2

INSTRUCTIONAL DEVELOPMENT SCRIPT CARD

SERIES TITLE:

PRODUCTION NEEDS:

LOG:
    FILM: DATE:
    CAMERA:
    METER: LOCATION:
    LENSE:

TAKE	LIGHT	SHUTTER	F/STOP	DISTANCE

REMARKS: The Roman numerial in the take box refers to the number of the roll of film and the Arabic number indicates the slide number on the roll of film. The letters in the light box mean: FL — front lighting, SL — side lighting, and BL — back lighting.

STORY BOARD   SLIDE NO.

MUSIC INTERVAL:

DESCRIPTION:

arranging the script cards, make sure the sequence tells the story and that it builds to a climax.

Now the film is ready to be shot. S.A.F.E. is a simple reminder for the photographer to set shutter speed, set aperture opening, focus camera and expose film. But all is for naught if the individual taking the pictures lacks a basic understanding of the principles of composition. Some of these will be discussed later in the paper.

With the shooting of the film, the photo essay compilation stage is reached. Now comes the hardest part for many individuals — selecting only the best slides. Next arrange the slides to match the story board, if necessary make any changes. Finalize the script and rehearse the photo essay. Evaluate individual shots, the sequence of the pictures and the narration, if used. Avoid needless details since they detract from the point you are making. Make your audience want what you have to teach or demonstrate.

Suggested Photo Essays

Numerous photo essay ideas should automatically come to mind to both students and teachers when careful consideration is given to the various phenomena or elements which comprise the physical and cultural environment. Differing agents of erosion, water or ice, could be treated. If the students live in an area that has experienced the effects of continental glaciation, contrasting depositional landforms due to water, eskers and lacustrine plains, or moving ice, terminal moraines or ground moraines could create a natural interest.

Students living in a community undergoing the impact of urban sprawl might focus in this direction. On the other hand, students interested in farming could concentrate on the life of a dairy farmer during a normal work day from sunrise to sunset. By contrast, others might be more concerned with discerning the different modes or types of farming in their county. However, students in an urban-industrial environment might be stimulated to trace the manufacturing process of a particular product, for example, an automobile (Ford's River Rouge Plant near Detroit). Today many students would probably be concerned with portraying the deterioration of the quality of their home environment in photo essay form. The idea could be attacked from the point of view of either a specific pollution problem, or the overall problem.

Not all photo essays need be instructive in nature. Instead, the primary purpose might focus on changing or influencing an individual's attitude or perception of some phenomena or problem in a local area. At the same time one should not rule out the possibility of a photo essay emphasizing strictly aesthetic values with other objectives taking a secondary role. For example, the color slide photo essay entitled, "A River: Source to Mouth," which I presented at the 1972 Annual Meeting of the National Council for Geographic Education in Milwaukee, had as its objective to increase the audience's appreciation of a river's beauty and a greater awareness of its entirety. Because of the nature of the color slide photo essay which was synchronized with a tape it naturally was excluded from this article. However, some brief comments concerning the photo essay and a series of black-white prints copied from the color slides are included for greater appreciation and understanding of the photo essay idea.

Originally, the photo essay was completed as partial requirements for a graduate course, Photography in Instruction, while completing doctoral work in geography at Michigan State University. The idea to concentrate on the Red Cedar River which flowed through the campus stemmed from the derogatory comments often made about the river by both faculty and students. Because such an attitude or perception bothered me, it was decided to emphasize the aesthetic values of the Red Cedar River. Therefore, the treatment chosen was a true photo essay where the pictures relate the story or idea without any narration. It was also determined that the color slide series should be in sequence in order to portray photographically the increasing size of the river. A 6 minute 55 second sequence of music, edited from Smetana's "The Moldau," provided the feeling of motion and contributed to the overall aesthetic value of the photo essay. In addition, the season of winter offered a captivating challenge to the photographer to illustrate the beauty and the unity of the river.

Due to the length of the river about 70-90 miles depending upon which of the three branches you followed, the Red Cedar River, a tributary of the Grand River, was divided into three segments for picture taking forays. In order to provide complete coverage of the river approximately 60 slides were taken with the shot locations primarily chosen at random. In taking pictures of the Red Cedar River it was extremely important to be aware of composition, so that the resulting views of the river would not appear static and similar. Therefore, the pictures were always composed keeping in mind, for example, angle of view, depth of field, advantages and disadvantages of a close-up over a long or medium shot, lighting and shadows. All of which suggests the art in photography is a key to a good photo essay.

Probably one of the most difficult problems encountered in the entire project centered around the synchronization of the slides to the music. The slides needed to be shown at varying intervals of time, because of the changing moods of the river and the music. Also, to hold the audience's attention the slides could not possibly remain on the screen the same length of time. Three options were available for solving the problem: (1) increase or decrease the number of slides included in the photo essay, (2) the timing sequence of the slides could be rearranged, since 5, 10 and 15 second intervals were utilized, and (3) lengthen or shorten the music edited from "The Moldau." In the final product 37 color slides were selected for the photo essay with 15 slides shown at 15 second intervals, 16 slides at 10 second intervals and 6 slides at 5 second intervals, but not necessarily in the order just indicated. The color slides were synchronized to the music by using a stereo tape recorder and recording the music on one channel and the beeps for operating the slide projector on the other channel.

Finally, the title slide was shot in a rather interesting way. Small black letters were cut out for the title and glued to a storm window. When the weather was appropriate with clear, blue skies the storm window was taken to a park in Lansing through which the river flowed. With the camera focused on the title the background of the river seen through the glass was naturally out of focus; thus, an effective title slide was produced. Of course, several title slides were shot at different f-stops and with different lenses to produce the desired effect.

Composition

Because composition pictorially supports content, unifies and focuses attention, it is the true art of photography.[5] Photographic composition refers to the arrangement of pictorially significant elements within the format of a predetermined frame. Accordingly, prominent objects, masses of light and dark, and horizontal and curved lines should appear in particular positions which suggest balance, form and rhythm. Nevertheless, composition cannot be reduced to a precise set of hard-and-fast rules, because it also depends upon the content of the idea and upon the objective and viewpoint of the photographer.[6] Hopefully most geographers would be concerned with improving their ability to effectively compose. An individual can learn to apply compositional principles by experimenting and by becoming more aware of how pictorial elements are properly arranged. In other words, the photographer needs to develop the art of seeing not only with the eyes, but also with the brain. If such an art is not learned, meaningful order will not evolve since the lens sees too much.[7]

The shape most pleasing to the eye is the rectangle. An artistically perfect rectangle is limited to one in which the diagonal of a square is equal to the base of a rectangle that maintains the original height of the square.[8] Kodak slides, 24 x 36mm, meet this criteria but not the square image of the instamatic. Moreover, the rectangular picture frame of Kodak's popular Kodachrome II-135 and Ektachrome X-135 slide films is an example of a most important rule of composition, *The Rule of Thirds*.

The Rule of Thirds

Too often the center of interest ends up in the geometric center of the frame, which results in a static "bulls-eye" composition. Applying *The Rule of Thirds* presupposes the mental division of the format into nine equal rectangles (Figure 3). An analysis of the work of professional photographers indicates a preference for locating the key objects or areas of primary interest near one of the four points which lie at the intersection of lines that divide the picture into thirds. Such

Figure 3
Favorable Locations for Centers of Interest in a Composition

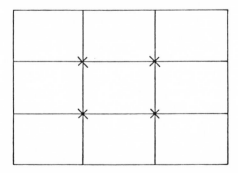

lines can also serve as guides for allocating space to different elements of the composition.[9] For example, in a distant landscape picture it is usually disturbing if the sky and land are divided equally; instead, one-third sky or one-third land is more pleasing (Figure 4 [page 118]). The same rule applies to marine pictures. Masses, the predominantly light or dark areas of a scene, should generally not be evenly

Figure 4

distributed between the right and the left halves of the picture or the scene will lose interest and lack balance.[10] But beware, applying *The Rule of Thirds* without concern for all the elements of composition and not just the center of interest will not necessarily always produce good pictures.[11]

Lines in a Composition

Balance in photo composition should cause the eye to be drawn to the center of interest. The photographer can provide leading lines or lines of force, whether real or imaginary, which not only will lead the viewer's eye to the center, but guide the eye in exploring the picture and also give a scene movement. Even as the relationship between light and dark areas contribute to the rhythm quality of photo composition, the linear quality of a picture also influences the structural elements of unity and rhythm. Unity means that all the component parts of a photograph are properly arranged in relation to the central feature.[12]

Real lines are actually seen, such as, fences, telephone wires, railroad tracks, edges of buildings, or separations between bare ground and vegetation. Imaginary lines are implied by the shape of an object, the apparent direction of movement of a vehicle or object and the relationships between actual lines.[13]

A landscape picture which expresses a feeling of peace or calmness will be dominated by horizontal lines (Figure 5).[14] On the other hand, vertical lines produce an impression of strength and dignity.[15] Whereas horizontal and vertical lines tend to suggest a feeling of staticness or monotony, slanting or diagonal lines generate an impression of movement and add to the dramatic effect. The significance of the diagonal line in photography is probably due to its

Figure 5

characteristic of being the longest straight line a picture frame can contain.[16] Furthermore, swift movement can be similarly alluded to with the use of radial, short angular and swirling lines (Figure 6).

Figure 6

But curved lines result in· a variety of interpretations, for example, long sweeping curves suggest grace. When curved the lines should follow a graceful "S" across the frame from foreground to background. Moreover, the photographer must utilize leading lines, real or imaginary, in as natural a manner as possible in guiding the eye about a picture. No matter what, the eye should not be led out of the picture, but if carried to the margin a way back should be provided.[17] Consequently, if misused real or imaginary lines may be disturbing and detract from the center of interest, rather than being a contributing element.

Although most of the landscape pictures that geographers shoot create a variety of problems for satisfactorily using leading lines or lines of force. Miller discusses certain standardized patterns into which the material of many pictures can be fitted in order to guarantee a reasonable arrangement.[18] For instance, if the dominating lines of a composition form roughly a triangle, with a horizontal or nearly horizontal base, the picture has the advantage of stability. In addition, this *triangular composition* will furnish a closed path to lead the eye over the subject matter with little danger of wandering out of the frame (Figure 7).

Figure 7

Other basic patterns are also capable of keeping the eye's attention within the picture. Arranging the most important elements of a picture in an ellipse or framing the picture with foreground materials results in *tunnel composition*. Such vista composition improves the feeling of depth. Meandering streams and curving roads arrange themselves in pleasing *spiral composition* (Figure 8). Perhaps too

Figure 8

often the photographer overlooks the significant contributions of large masses of light and shade for attracting and holding the viewer's attention. Furthermore, to accomplish this carrying power quality requires working early or late in the day when the shadows are long and soft. All the above devices are employed to create an illusion of depth or perspective, in other words, the process of transforming three-dimensional space to a flat plane.

Framing

Even though the geographer's landscape pictures impart perspective by nature, many flat uninteresting scenes could be improved by adding a touch of foreground detail, framing, to foster the illusion of depth (Figure 9). Because

Figure 9

framing can produce a strong feeling of perspective to the composition, the photographer needs to avoid excessive amounts of establishing elements, such as leaves and tree branches, which could detract from the main purpose. Most importantly the establishing elements should be relatively unobstructive and appropriate to the scene. Meanwhile, the photographer must avoid applying similar establishing elements for most of his pictures. In addition, by remembering to always expose for the principal part of the scene, never for the establishing elements, the framing elements will appear silhouette, semi-silhouette or partial shadow.

Good composition also requires composing in depth—foreground, middle ground and far ground (Figure 10). Such an awareness contributes to visual variety, because the photographer is frequently changing the compositional pattern. Another factor, choice of shooting distance, not only influences the perspective, but also determines the primary emphasis within the picture format. Consequently, the photographer's purpose affects the choice of shooting distance; therefore, the important thing to remember is not to include too much in the frame (Figure 11 [page 124]). As was mentioned earlier in the paper, the three available options for shooting distance are the close-up, the medium shot and the long shot. In contrast, obtaining the best viewpoint is also affected by the photographer realizing that a step to the right or the left, or a slight bending of

Figure 10

the knees, or a change of focal length (35mm, 50mm, 135mm, or 200mm lens) may eliminate an obstruction within the picture frame or cause the perspective lines to emphasize the center of interest.

Particularly in a photographic essay where the story is intended to live in the viewer's mind, long shots and changing viewpoints should be exploited to draw attention to the center of interest in a sequence of pictures. Another means of emphasizing the center of interest and adding human interest to a static picture would be to place a foreground figure in profile or gazing toward the important element of a scene. At the same time, the image of the person supplies a familiar element within the picture's composition which also, then, establishes a scale relationship for the viewer's judgment of depth.[19] Other familiar objects which might serve the photographer's purpose are automobiles, fences, animals, buildings (See Figure 4 [page 118]).

In conclusion, the rules and principles of good composition are alterable and can be changed either to please or disturb the viewer. At the same time, they are only a substitute for good taste and an intelligent eye. But if the pictures which are used in a photo essay or in general classroom use lack good composition they will not produce the desired audience reaction. Instead, the poor composition will disrupt the emotional experience of the audience and the educational value of the pictures. By remembering not to place the center of interest in the geometric center of the frame, which results in a static "bulls-eye" composition, a major step will have been taken to improve the quality of the slides taken by geographers. Hopefully with the utilization of better quality slides and an instructional media technique like the photo essay, the geography teacher will have a teaching tool which will turn on the students when he or she turns off the lights.

Figure 11

Footnotes

¹See, for example, Simon Baker, "Some Photographic Techniques for Geographers," *Professional Geographer*, Vol. XIII (May, 1961), pp. 23-26; John V. Baltram and Charles B. Varney, *Geography Via Projected Media*, Do It This Way No. 3 (Normal, Ill,: National Council for Geographic Education, 1968); Howard F. Gregor, "Slide-Projection Techniques in the Geography Class," *Journal of Geography*, Vol. LV (September, 1956), pp. 298-303; Paul F. Griffin and Ronald L. Chatham, "The Still Picture in Geography Instruction," *Audiovisual Instruction*, Vol. XI (May, 1966), pp. 355-360; E. Willard Miller, "Use of Color Slides," *Journal of Geography*, Vol. LXIV (October, 1965), pp. 304-307; and Wayne R. White, "Slides As a Teaching Aid in Geography," *Audiovisual Instruction*, Vol. XI (May, 1966), pp. 352-354.

[2]H. J. Walls, *How Photography Works* (New York; Macmillan Company, 1959), p. 306.

[3]Carl W. Miller, *Principles of Photographic Reproduction* (New York: Macmillan Company, 1942), p. 72.

[4]Robert B. Rhode and Floyd H. McCall, *Introduction to Photography* (New York: The Macmillan Company, 1965), p. 44.

[5]Harry Sternberg, *Composition* (New York: Pitman Publishing Corporation, 1958).

[6]Andreas Feininger, *The Creative Photographer* (Englewood Cliffs, N.J.: Prentice-Hall, Inc., 1955), pp. 289-290 and Rhode and McCall, *op. cit.*, pp. 32-33.

[7]Rhode and McCall, *op. cit.*, pp. 34-35.

[8]Notes from a graduate course, *Photography in Instruction*, taught by Dr. Robert Kline, Michigan State University, Winter Quarter, 1968.

[9]Miller, *op. cit.*, p. 74.

[10]*Ibid.*, pp. 74-75.

[11]Rhode and McCall, *op, cit.*, p. 45.

[12]Marcel Natkin, *Photography and the Art of Seeing* (London: Fountain Press, 1948), p. 20.

[13]Rhode and McCall, *op. cit.*, pp. 45-46.

[14]Natkin, *op. cit.*, p. 28.

[15]Julian M. Blair, *Practical and Theoretical Photography* (New York: Pitman Publishing Corporation, 1945), pp. 179 and 182.

[16]Natkin, *op. cit.*, p. 28.

[17]Miller, *op. cit.*, pp. 75 and 77.

[18]*Ibid.*, pp. 77-80.

[19]Rhode and McCall, *op. cit.*, pp. 40-42.

THE CASE FOR FILMSTRIPS:
PRODUCING FILMSTRIPS IN
THE CLASSROOM
Doris P. Miller

Just what place should film making have in the English classroom? How effective is it, *really*, in helping students to become literate and articulate? Is film making just another educational gimmick, one more expensive fad to help teacher and student avoid the difficult but "meaningful" learning tasks that lead to command of communication skills? Having just completed my twenty-second "production," I can say with some authority that there can be few better ways to teach reading, writing, and oral expression on the secondary level than working with students in producing sound filmstrips and slide-sound productions. My enthusiasm for filmstrip making has grown over the past seven years (See *English Journal*, February 1968) because of the following:

1. Filmstrips are relatively inexpensive to produce and they become valuable teaching aids in succeeding classes.

2. Producing a filmstrip involves *all* of the students in the class, utilizing individual talents and encouraging creativity. The artists have a chance to paint illustrations that are photographed to become additional frames. The "scholars" (and even reluctant readers) are motivated to do research papers that might become part of the script. The musicians and the technicians have an opportunity to work with equipment, music, and sound effects. The actors have prominent roles in the taping.

3. Reading skills are improved as students are forced to read very closely the literature they'll be translating into film. They learn to look beyond story line for characterization, setting, style, and theme. They become concerned with the HOW, the WHERE, and the WHY rather than just the WHAT of a story.

4. Vocabulary is broadened as new film terminology is introduced. Students become more "cinema-literate" as many movie making terms are applied to this less sophisticated film form. Their own struggles make them aware of the problems and special techniques of professional film making.

5. Ability to work in groups is increased as each small group project must be completed for the success of the entire production. A feeling of comradeship in a common cause develops. There is no derision when someone fluffs a line in recording the sound track

Reprinted by permission of the author and the National Council of Teachers of English from *English Journal* 66 (October 1977):70-72.

because the would-be scoffer might be the next one to "goof." The valuable old saw that "everyone makes mistakes" (including the teacher) is brought home effectively. Patience and perseverence become the watchwords.

6. Listening skills develop as students listen to the sounds of their own voices, the sounds of their fellow students, the sounds of the author's words, the sounds of their contributions to the script, and the sound of music and effects to be used for background.

7. Most important of all, from my own point of view, is that in producing a filmstrip students increase their composition skills. I have found no better way to get across to my classes the importance of transition, unity, emphasis, mood, tone, coherence, balance, contrast—elements of style to improve their writing. And my constant admonition to "be specific" becomes clear when their penchant for generalities is likened to extreme long shots while specific points are similar to close-ups visually. They soon learn that a paper composed only of sweeping generalities is as lacking in impact as a film with no close-ups.

How, then, specifically, can the above goals of English teaching be achieved through this relatively new teaching technique? Perhaps a report on our most recent production, a twenty-eight minute sound-slide show based on Alan Paton's beautiful novel of South Africa, *Cry the Beloved Country*, might make this clear. My own interest in re-reading the novel was aroused by a summer trip to South Africa where I took pictures "on location" in Johannesburg. Some of these became the nucleus of our film. How to get ninth graders interested in a story whose hero is an old black preacher *could* have been difficult, but my own enthusiasm and the prospect of their becoming film makers of-a-sort proved to be sufficient motivation for even the most skeptical.

First we went over the book's introduction together in class so that the author's purpose became clear at the outset. Students were then assigned to read the book at home. I provided a ditto of things to be aware of as they were reading, ideas that would be a part of the class discussion to precede any script writing.

In class we read together and dramatized *Lost in the Stars*, the musical version of the novel, listening to the music, discussing the lyrics, and comparing and contrasting the two literary forms. We then had a showing of the black and white film which added another dimension to their understanding. Next we read reviews of the book (this was their introduction to the *Book Review Digest*), the play, and the *new* movie version. By the time we had examined the novel, the play, and the film the students had a firm grasp of the material and were ready to begin their filmstrip.

After seeing the movie the students became aware of some of the problems involved in translating literature into film. What would be our point of view? What characters and scenes would have to be eliminated? How could we get across the beauty of the language and the essence of the message without belaboring points? How could we suggest ideas through images?

Buzz sessions and panel discussions on the above helped bring ideas into focus (while providing opportunities for oral expression and listening). Each student then decided what aspect of the book and play he would be responsible for covering: character, setting, plot, theme, or style. They worked in groups on these areas — some doing research, some finding pictures to photograph, some finding dialogue and descriptive passages to illustrate.

Next came the selection of scenes to be portrayed visually. In addition to the slides taken in Johannesburg, we needed a title frame, an end frame, some dramatic scenes from the story and some kind of visual representation of symbols and main ideas. One hang-up was where to find a picture of a tityhoya bird. When our search proved in vain I wrote to Alan Paton himself asking for help. Would he please provide us with some information about this South African bird? He very graciously responded, and we discovered that a picture of one of our own plovers would be close enough. The artists in the class provided water colors or pastels that photographed beautifully — after they were cautioned about avoiding white spaces that make a glare when shown on the screen. (All drawing paper should be "washed" with a soft pastel shade before painting.)

Some of the most effective art work showed the many contrasts in the book in a kind of split screen effect: a white fist and black hands in prayerful supplication; a church altar and a gun; a heart and lightning (love and fear); a home and a shack. One student drew a map of the locale, another, the railroad tracks to Johannesburg. Our title frame was a close-up view of the title page of the paperback and the end frame was a student-drawing of a black hand and a white hand clasped in friendship. In fact, the artistic output was so great that we ended with ninety-one frames, far too many for our half-hour filmstrip. So, next, of course, was the problem of editing.

To make this easier all of the slides were numbered and identified on ditto sheets which students followed as the slides were shown to the class. Each student then contracted to write the script for at least five frames. (I volunteered to write any that were not selected.) Unfortunately some frames were more popular than others, but almost all were chosen by someone in the class.

One of the students' biggest problems in writing the script was to avoid the infantile Show and Tell format. "This is a picture of ... " would of course, be a redundancy. Why tell the audience what they can actually see? Why put into words what is already visually apparent? Words had to expand on, further illuminate the picture, add another dimension, suggest, help evoke a mood and maybe (miraculously) elicit empathy.

Another difficulty was the students' inclination to merely retell the story. Since plot is so negligible in *Cry the Beloved Country* this type of script would be worthless as a study aid for future classes. Rather, the focus had to be on theme, philosophy, characters, setting, and style. Motivation, inner conflicts, social conflicts — all had to be explored. Passages from the book and play were quoted to bring out the theme of love and fear as motivating forces, and descriptive passages were read aloud for an appreciation of the lovely cadences of the Zulu tongue as Paton captured them.

"Many hands make light work" does *not* apply to a stable of twenty-five script writers! With the entire class participating in the writing the achievement of some kind of unity can become a herculean task. But what a way to get across the importance of transition!

After each student had written his five frames, the editors and I circled the most important ideas in each and returned them to the authors to write in fewer words. They learned the hard way what their teachers had been telling them for years — it's much easier to write a long paper than it is to write a short one saying the same thing. For their revisions they were given only a half sheet of paper for each frame. Some frames, they discovered, needed only sound effects or a fragment of music to convey the message effectively.

After these revisions had been made we attacked the problem of transitions. The slides were arranged on the slide sorter in sequence so that each student could see the frames that would precede and follow his. We went over the most commonly used transitional words and phrases and discussed more subtle ways of using linking expressions than putting them obtrusively at the beginning of paragraphs — such as tucking them into the middle of sentences, or using a musical bridge or sound effect. (Movie production has the edge here with dissolves and wipes, but smooth transition between slides can give even a series of stills some of the fluidity of a movie.)

Next, the slides and script had to be edited down to seventy frames because we were aiming for a half-hour show to fit comfortably into our forty-two minute class periods. Here the students learned some of the suffering of Hollywood writers and actors when their scenes land on the cuttingroom floor.

With the slides and script completed, we moved on to the taping of the sound track. Copies of the script were passed out and volunteers were asked for the reading of each frame. Everyone had some part in the recording. Dialogue had been included for dramatic effect so these parts had to be cast. I arbitrarily selected the best voices for the key roles, but some frames required several voices so there was ample opportunity for everyone to be recorded. Our technicians included the boy running the tape recorder, the boy on the record player and mixer, the sound effects man, the bell ringer (who indicated when the next frame was to be shown), and the director who was in charge, not only of getting interpretation and correct volume from the participants, but also of keeping the rest of the class quiet.

Besides dubbing in much of the lovely Kurt Weil music we used sound effects of crowds, birds, church bells, and gun shots. The music proved to be a new experience for the rock addicts in the class. They learned that the lyrics of a song can have *meaning* and can serve the dramatic functions of advancing the plot, characterizing, establishing mood or setting, or underscoring theme. (This in itself made the project worthwhile to me!)

Our completed filmstrip runs twenty-eight minutes, and will be a helpful teaching device for students who will read the book and play this year. Student evaluations at the end of the school year placed filmstrip making at the top of the Most Valuable Learning Experiences list. It becomes evident, then, that students who make filmstrips may become cinema-literate, and they may develop sensory perception and social awareness, but they also learn how to read, speak, and write.

VII

VISUAL LITERACY PROGRAMS

During the past ten years there has been a notable growth in the effort by educators to develop course work that will increase youngsters' visual awareness of the objects that surround them in their everyday lives. Visual literacy programs have either been attached to existing subject areas or have been organized as a separate unit of instruction within the curriculum.

The lead article to this section by Samuel B. Ross, Jr. clarifies the meaning of the term "visual literacy" and provides the reader with examples of how students are stimulated to interact with their environment and others by exploring the full range of nonprint production. Frank M. Young in "Visual Literacy Today and Tomorrow" discusses the successes he had with designing a visual communications art class for junior high school students. He sets forth the idea of the need to teach youngsters using familiar objects so as to prepare them "to work and create in their time—the future." Jill C. Dardig in "A Visual Literacy Program for Deaf Students" describes a program developed by the Northeast Regional Media Center for the Deaf designed to teach middle school-aged deaf students how to communicate using visual media. The problems experienced by the hearing-impaired student in developing language and communication skills are explained, along with the unique features of this program, in an effort to remedy these deficits.

VISUAL LITERACY – A NEW CONCEPT?   Samuel B. Ross, Jr.

In the days of the little one-room schoolhouse, individualized instruction, flexible grouping, student tutors, self-help programs, and "home-made" instructional materials were integral parts of every teacher's daily program. But as society progressed it became more mechanized, more specialized, more departmentalized, and in many cases less effective. Textbooks were improved, teacher's manuals were expanded, and a wide variety of commercial teaching aids were developed and distributed. However, along with these technological gains came an increasing awareness that education was not meeting the needs of many youngsters.

"New" techniques were tried, new approaches were developed. We now find ourselves trying innovations which, in reality, can be traced back to the master teacher in her one-room schoolhouse. What is apparent, however, is that the approach to educating the masses must be a multi-sensory, multi-disciplinary one, flexible and realistic in its methods and goals.

From the vast proliferation of materials on the educational scene has come a renewed emphasis on the value of and need for a more visual approach to learning. This concept has evolved to become what is now known as visual literacy. It would be fruitless to debate whether this concept is an innovation or simply the repetition of what has been successful in the past. What is important is to determine its value for today's society, and to define its role in our educational system.

Ours is the age of mass media. Ours is a mobile, volatile society. Our schools, if they are to be effective, must recognize this and deal with the changes that are so rapidly taking place. For the pre-school youngster who has grown up with "Sesame Street," a visual approach to learning has already been deeply ingrained by the time he/she enters school. How sterile the three Rs must seem in comparison to the viable, living alphabet he/she met on "Sesame Street."

If educators are to effect change, the place to begin is in the early grades with the youngest learners, with those who have not yet been "turned off" by repeated failure or mediocrity.

The controversy rages still over the pros and cons of the effect of TV on our youth. S. I. Hayakawa, leading semanticist, in a talk presented to the American Psychological Association stressed that an important – and probably the most destructive – element of TV watching is that the observer has no interaction with it. Children sitting in front of their TV sets "get no experience in influencing behavior or being influenced in return.... Is there any connection between this fact and the sudden appearance in the past few years of an enormous number of young people from educated and middle-class families who find it difficult or impossible to relate to anyone – and therefore drop out?" Hayakawa compared

Reprinted by permission of the author and the Association for Educational Communications and Technology from *Audiovisual Instruction* 17 (May 1972):12-15.

TV to a powerful sorcerer who snatches a child away from his parents for three to four hours a day, about 22,000 hours by the time he reaches 18.

Whether one agrees wholly with Hayakawa is not at issue here. What is pertinent is that our children are exposed daily to the good as well as the "evil" of television, and that this material influences their concept formation. How we react and respond to this challenge is the issue. How we utilize the technology and know-how of the media to make our teaching more effective is what is important and pertinent.

When we speak of visual literacy, we refer to the numerous techniques used by people to communicate with each other in nonverbal ways. We mean body language, art forms, pantomime, graphic expression, filmed expression, picture story expression, and many others. When we say that this is another approach to educating youngsters, we are speaking in terms of those who cannot learn visually, as well as those who will not.

It is a widely accepted truism that with unmotivated youngsters, or hostile ones, the traditional program is inadequate and ineffective. These are the children who will not—or who think they cannot—learn. Many are middle-class children, but it is in the slums, where education has truly failed, that some startling and dramatic results have been observed. Often these results are due to the work of community action groups. One example was the establishment, in 1967, of a Youth Communications Center in the slums of the South Bronx. The director of this project, Melvin Roman, felt that where everything else had failed, perhaps art should be tried. It was his goal to foster a sense of community in the slums by establishing a youth communications and community action center. He envisioned using film techniques to develop news and special interest stories, playing them back as a means of self-discovery and self-confrontation. He also incorporates drama, dance, music, painting, and design, but the prime emphasis is placed on film because of its strong appeal for youth and its great interest for audiences.

In his proposal for the project, Roman said:

> Training in the filmmaking arts and group experience in neighborhood film production will appeal strongly to the adolescent's search for a meaningful cause and positive identity. Communicating successfully and contributing to meaningful social action will go far toward the establishment of autonomy and social competence. Though the experience might lead to professionalism for a few, the discovery of individual talent is secondary to the basic goals of using the communication arts for individual and social change.... Communication—almost always a problem in adolescence—may be especially difficult for slum children without literate and articulate examples to follow.

How to incorporate this concept of visual literacy into the school curriculum, how to breathe new life into the daily routine, how to eliminate some of the "crippled readers" in our schools, these are the problems we now face and must solve. No one method or set of materials will work for 100 percent of the children. But for all children, except for those relatively few who require institutional care, there is some method that will bring success.

As part of a pilot project designed to approach this problem of reading and visual-verbal communication, a group of students in a residential independent school were provided with easily operated cameras and film and, after a brief discussion of the mechanics of picture taking, were sent out to take some pictures. Since one of the goals of the study was to use the camera as a tool for developing a new form of self-expression, no subjects were suggested or themes given for the students. The pictures they shot were solely of their own choosing, and the results proved to be very enlightening. In many cases, a theme was apparent. For some students, their friends filled their pictures; one boy included only inanimate objects in this collection. These photographs were visual statements by the children of things that were important to them. They provided valuable insights into each child's world as he saw and experienced it.

Next, the students were asked to use their cameras to take photo sequences. This time they were made aware that there was to be a theme and a logical sequencing. Again, much valuable information about the children was obtained. Indications of their awareness of the progression of time, of logical movement from one phase to another and of causal relationships between stimulus and response were shown. Equally significant were the themes revealed in the series. Some were of social import, others were of purely personal value; in every case, however, the student was revealing some very definite self information. The photographs were used as bases for group discussions and for points of departure during individual student-teacher conferences.

After having attempted a variety of techniques and effects with the still camera, the students were ready to work with the moving picture camera and its almost limitless possibilities. They were encouraged to experiment and try out many techniques, and again the results were both rewarding to the students and revealing about them. One boy, wishing to express how he felt when things begin to close in on him, sat on a merry-go-round and had someone push him around, first slowly, then faster. The result — an exciting and expressive flash of color and movement of form — pleased him and gave him the motivation to try for other novel effects.

The films were by the students and for the students. This autonomy was perhaps the most critical factor in the success of the project, for it provided for freedom of choice of subject, of equipment, of timing. In short, it provided for complete freedom and autonomy by the student. For interested, motivated youngsters the project was a success; for the unmotivated or hostile ones, it was a revelation and a breakthrough.

From the students' point of view, the filmmaking experience was both stimulating and personally rewarding. The act of producing a finished product — a movie — was in itself an accomplishment. This was direct positive reinforcement for them. They felt very special and privileged to have been selected for the project, and took great pride in their creations. They learned many of the technical skills of filmmaking which some day may prove to be of value to them. They were introduced to an entirely new realm of self-expression, which for some may become a vocation or hobby. Above all, their feelings of personal worth and value seemed to rise as they shared their films with their peers, parents and teachers. Many educational goals had been realized, and in an involved, exciting, innovative way, not just for the bright and the eager students, but even for the defeated, reluctant, "crippled" ones.

A natural outgrowth of the movie project was the use of closed-circuit videotape equipment. Some of the advantages of this media are readily seen. Instant playback affords immediate reinforcement and provides numerous opportunities for discussion. It helps develop the ability to critique, to analyze, to keep to the subject, to detect and correct errors as they occur. The added advantage of audio accompaniment lends an intensified sense of reality to the film. The student's fluency in the use of language can be detected. Vocabulary can be analyzed and improved. It is a true experience in self-confrontation for students to watch themselves.

One can go on endlessly citing the activities which are inherent in this concept of visual literacy. And one can return to the days of the one-room schoolhouse with its master teacher, utilizing every modality, every discipline, every media within grasp, and the question will still remain unresolved: "Visual literacy—a new concept?" But it really is irrelevant whether our concept is new, old or a combination of both. For in the final analysis what is important is whether it can help us as educators to do the job entrusted to us, to meet the academic and emotional needs of our youngsters. It is this writer's opinion that the answer must be yes.

VISUAL LITERACY TODAY AND TOMORROW

Frank M. Young

"But I thought that we were going to sketch, paint and write reports."

This comment was one of the many which I encountered during the summer Junior High Art Camp. I realized that the visual curriculum that I had developed would be different from a junior high school art curriculum—but I had not realized how different it would be.

The purpose of the camp was to reinforce the basic concepts of line, shape, color, texture, and space through instruction in the uses of visual and related media; i.e., photograms, photographs, light media, animated film making, light and shadow modulation (three-dimensional folded paper forms), and finally computer graphics. Complementing our studio courses, we offered a course in survey of photography which coordinated the other areas by showing examples of work done by professional artists executed in media that junior high students have experienced in classrooms or at home.

In the photography class, the students experienced what was, for most, a new media, a new means of expression. Unless one has experienced or taught photography, one cannot imagine the excitement that the student encounters when he watches his first photograph appear in the developer. Pride of authorship is plain to see.

In order to learn the properties of light sensitive emulsion, which is a basic element of photography, we began with photograms. Photopaper exposed to light will record the varied intensities of light sources in black, white, and gray values. At this time we stress composition and consciously teach for transfer from traditional media. Maholy-Nagy, in *Vision in Motion*, stated, "The photogram can be called the key to photography because every good photograph must possess the same fine gradations between the white and black extremes as the photogram."

During the camp, each student constructed his own pinhole camera. Many of the students were amazed at the quality of photographs that they obtained from a "cardboard box."

In the light-media class, the students are first introduced to light as an art medium; demonstrations and lectures were given explaining the primary light colors and how they differ from pigment primaries. Each student experienced the making of transparencies and saw the effect of polarized light upon their 2x2-inch compositions when they were projected on a screen. The campers also experimented with da-glo paints under the effect of black light.

From my experiences in teaching in the public schools, I have found the junior high age student very much interested in paper folding; therefore, our light-and-shadow modulation class makes use of paper-folding techniques and relates this to our curriculum. The function of the light modulator is to catch,

Reprinted by permission of the author and *Arts & Activities* 73 (February 1973):44-45.

reflect, and modulate light. A flat surface does not modulate—it only reflects. But any surface composed of concave-convex surfaces reflects light with varied intensity depending upon its substance and position in regard to the light source. The effect that light has upon three-dimensional form is of utmost importance to the visual artist.

Our most popular class was animated film-making. The students were divided into groups and a total of fourteen films were produced during the ten days at camp. The students used traditional media and techniques to execute their films. It required thought, cooperation, and coordination on the part of the students. Although a majority of the students had never used a movie camera previously, they experienced little difficulty in setting up lights, taking readings, and operating the single-frame capacity cameras.

The newest addition to the curriculum was the course in computer drawing. To my knowledge, this was one of the first computer classes in design applications of art offered to students anywhere in the country.

The last day was spent preparing and presenting an exhibition and light-media show. This gave the students and parents a chance to see what had been accomplished.

The camp was a new experience for the students, and, at the beginning, they reacted normally: they were skeptical, even slightly apprehensive. As the program progressed, they began to relax and became involved with the curriculum. I felt that a majority of the students had not only enjoyed themselves, but also had learned a great deal.

The key phrase in art education today is: visual education—visual literacy. Can you teach for, and attain greater, visual literacy by using the same methods, materials, and processes that were being advocated 20 years ago? I think not. Art education should be considered a vital part of the student's total development.

As the art teacher, you have learned in the past and are teaching in the present. You have an obligation to prepare your students to work and create in their time—the future.

A VISUAL LITERACY PROGRAM
FOR DEAF STUDENTS

Jill C. Dardig

The generation of students presently in our educational system are growing up in a unique environment—they have had continuous and overwhelming exposure to visual media and messages through television, film, photography, graphics, and other manifestations of the current technology. Outside of school, these media have been ever-present influences in their lives. But, for most students, their relationships to the media both in and out of school has remained a passive one. They customarily have been in the position of being the recipients in a one-way process; of watching but not participating. In recent years, the recognition of the one-sidedness of this situation has lead many educators to express their concern that communication through the visual media should be a two-way process with students taking an active role.

The teachers, media specialists, and researchers who have been involved in the visual literacy movement are showing their concern in a practical way by developing programs which teach students to actively manipulate the tools of technology for educational purposes. Although the majority of visual literacy programs have been designed for use with average school populations, the potential for extending their use to benefit students with special educational needs is beginning to be explored.

One such special population, hearing impaired and deaf students, is particularly dependent on visual communication skills for learning about their environment and for sharing their responses with their teachers, parents, and peers. Educators of the deaf are acutely aware that visual cues are crucial to the deaf child's development of communication skills, and that the deaf child needs continuous visual stimulation and training in order to develop this sense to its fullest utility.

Teachers, media personnel, and others have long sought to improve the quality and effectiveness of education of the deaf by using mediated visual means. But although mediated as well as non-mediated visual language instruction forms the dominant segment of a deaf child's classroom experience, deaf children have an extremely difficult time acquiring both receptive and expressive functional language and communication skills. An additional problem, low levels of student interaction, is an outgrowth of the language deficit.

A visual literacy approach, which allows students to express those things which they may not be able to verbalize using visual means, is one way of starting to deal with some of the language and communication problems which are common with deaf children. However, despite the fact that media have long been an integral part of education of the deaf, there has been a noticeable lack of visual literacy programs and materials geared especially for deaf students.

Reprinted by permission of the author and the Association for Educational Communications and Technology from *Audiovisual Instruction* 19 (October 1974):24-27.

In response to this lack of visual literacy materials for deaf students, the Northeast Regional Media Center for the Deaf (NRMCD) developed a Visual Communications Program designed to teach middle-school aged deaf students how to communicate specific information to their peers using visual media such as graphics, photography, and videotape. In addition to teaching specific visual communication skills, the program was designed to facilitate high levels of student interaction and participation, and to function as a set of stimulus materials for language development.

Receptive and expressive visual communication skills are shaped in this program using a set of 42 curricular objectives and activities described in a teacher's guide. These are supplemented by corresponding materials which include 68 overhead transparencies, 20 black-and-white photographs, 10 color slides, and assorted commercial materials. The program was specially designed to incorporate the following features:

Objective-Based

The NRMCD Visual Communications Program is objective-based. That is, the entire curriculum is guided by a set of behavioral objectives keyed to sets of activities, suggested teaching procedures, and materials which are designed to facilitate the attainment of each corresponding objective. Objectives range from expressing emotions and communicating environments using drawings and collages, to telling a simple story using a series of photos, to creating an animated film to convey a particular theme.

Successful Communication

The important question, "How will we know if visual communication is successful?" is a major concern of this program. In order to determine to what extent each student project, no matter how simple, has met the stated objective by communicating the student's intended message to his/her peers, a "successful communication" test is used. For the purpose of the NRMCD program, "successful communication" is operationally defined as "the information presented is correctly identified by at least one-half of the class." After completion of the projects suggested by each objective, each student presents his/her work to the class, which tries to identify the intended message. Thus, successful communication is determined by the relative criterion of peer response rather than by any predetermined and arbitrary standards.

The application of this test is critical for the success of the program because through this vehicle students are able to immediately evaluate their own efforts and to obtain useful feedback on how to make improvements. The program is structured so that students are likely to succeed in completing the majority of objectives.

Focus on Environment

Most of the activities require children to become involved with their in- and out-of-school environments, both as observers and as communicators of information. This focus on the child's environment serves to stimulate active student responses using new channels of communication based on a content area with which the student is already familiar.

Individualization

This program relies on the individual teacher to adapt the program — both in presentation of and response to the materials — to the level of each particular class. Several strategies are used for this purpose. The lower portions of all transparencies are left blank, allowing the teacher to clarify or extend the concepts presented whenever necessary; the teacher is encouraged to re-order, omit, or add objectives of his/her own choosing; and a section of each objective worksheet designated as "Individualization Strategies" includes alternative activities and porcedures for implementing each objective.

For these reasons, the ages and achievement levels of participating students can span a wider range than if the program did not encourage this kind of flexibility.

Active Student Response

Activities and visual stimulus materials are designed to promote active response on the part of the students. Channels are continuously provided for each student to respond in a variety of visual and verbal modes including writing, oral and/or total communication, and mediated communication. This particular feature of the program is built in so that the teacher can continuously monitor student progress toward the completion of objectives; student interest can be more easily maintained through active participation; and students, who have long been passive recipients of mediated messages via print advertisements, television, and film, can begin to take an active role in the media communication process.

Interaction

Since this curriculum is concerned with shaping new and useful communication skills, peer interaction is an important component of the program. Classroom activities are structured so that there are constant opportunities for students to exchange ideas in a variety of different sized groups through discussions, cooperative group activities and projects, and in using the "successful communication" test procedure.

The field test and evaluation of the prototype version of the NRMCD Visual Communications Program involved approximately 100 students aged 9-20 years in 13 classes for the deaf in 12 different schools during the spring of 1974. The results of the evaluation showed that students consistently completed objectives at very high levels of proficiency. In fact, the majority of students successfully completed objectives at an average rate of 85-99 percent. In addition, teacher reactions to the program were strongly positive. Many reported that students showed improvements in written and oral or sign language, especially in terms of variety, sequence, and fluency of response; higher rates of student interaction; and high levels of student interest and participation. The evaluation also served to pinpoint several areas which might be the focus of further research.

Many of the teachers who participated in the field test are planning to integrate the NRMCD Visual Communications Program into their standard school curricula. The program is currently being revised and is being considered by the National Center for Educational Media and Materials for the Handicapped for distribution this fall.

Several activities involving the use of videotape allowed students to be actively involved in the process of television production. A young student cameraman is pictured.

Students experimented with photography and gained new perspectives on their environment. The focus on out-of-school environment served to stimulate active student responses using new channels of communications.

A collage based on the theme "communication" is created by a student. In presenting the completed work to the class, the child will be able to evaluate his efforts and to gain useful feedback from his peers.

BIBLIOGRAPHY

Association for Educational Communications and Technology (AECT). 1126 16th Street, NW, Washington, DC 20036.

The Association has a variety of print and nonprint about visual literacy materials and programs. Write to the organization for an annotated listing of their publications.

The Audio-Visual Equipment Directory (198-). Fairfax, VA: National Audio-Visual Association (NAVA).

This annual publication is a listing and description of hardware available from members and nonmembers of NAVA, the trade organization of the AV industry. The directory is designed to help buyers make cost-effective decisions on the purchase and use of equipment. No implication is made that the directory includes all equipment available. Endorsement is not implied, nor does omission imply lack of approval.

Audiovisual Market Place: A Multimedia Guide. New York: Bowker, 1980.

A compendium of nonprint, *AVMP* is updated every year and includes complete information on audiovisual software and hardware. The reference section contains a calendar for nonprint events during the year, reference books and directories, periodicals and trade journals, national, regional, and state associations, funding sources, awards, festivals, and a glossary of terms.

"A-V Equipment Self-Instruction Packets." Eleven sound filmstrips. Random House Miller-Brody, 400 Hahn Road, Westminster, MD 21157. n.d.

These self-instructional packets are intended for use by students or teachers who wish to gain competency in equipment operation. Step-by-step instructions along with a diagram of the equipment make the units useful. Equipment covered includes the cassette recorder, record player, filmstrip viewer, super 8mm film loop projector, opaque projector, slide carousel projector, and reel-to-reel tape recorder.

Bell, Jo Ann. "Media Mix: Students Learn about Books from Tapes." *Top of the News* 27 (June 1971):388-94.

In this article, the author discusses the way a district goes about building a personal collection of book talks available on audiotape. She gives information on preparation and duplication of the tapes, reasons for preparing the tapes, and procedures for using the tapes in the media centers.

Brown, J. W., Lewis, R. B., and Harcleroad, F. F. *AV Instruction: Technology, Media, and Methods.* 5th ed. New York: McGraw-Hill, 1977.

This is a textbook that presents "an overview of media used in instruction and communication." It may also be used as a reference tool for teachers and librarians wishing to locate information on the role of media in various instructional programs, on selection, production, and use of individual media, or on future trends of media and telecommunication systems. Of particular value is the reference section, which covers such items as operating audiovisual equipment, duplicating processes, photographic equipment and techniques, physical facilities, classified directory of sources, and references.

Brown, James W., and Lewis, Richard B. *AV Instructional Manual for Independent Study*. 5th ed. New York: McGraw-Hill, 1977.

The manual may be used as a guide for creating instructional materials, for selection and use of ready-made materials, or for equipment operation. Also included are performance checklists for commonly-used equipment. Each unit in the manual is concise with specific resources to the textbook, *AV Instruction*, for additional reading. Black-and-white illustrations and line drawings enhance the text.

"Creating Slide/Tape Programs." Sound filmstrip. Washington, DC: AECT, 1980.

The filmstrip with audiocassette describes the process of producing a slide/tape program. Ideas on scripting, photography, and audio production are covered.

"The Creative Eye." Three sound filmstrips. Society for Visual Education, 1345 Diversey Parkway, Chicago, IL 60614. n.d.

The series of filmstrips challenges students to see familiar places and things in new ways. Photographs encourage children to use their imaginations.

Dondis, D. A. *A Primer of Visual Literacy*. Cambridge, MA: MIT Press, 1973.

This handbook is a basic guide to an understanding of the role visual literacy plays in the communication process and how it is displayed in the visual arts.

Eastman Kodak Company. Education Markets Services, Rochester, NY 14650.

The Eastman Kodak Company is continuously revising and adding to their print and nonprint holdings for circulation and use by teachers and library media specialists. Costs for loan or purchase are typically inexpensive. Many items are free, such as *Montage: Imagination in Learning*, a newsletter for educators showing students using and producing their own nonprint; *Teaching Tips from Teachers!*, a compilation of ideas sent in by teachers of their methods of using photography in the classroom; and *Your Programs from Kodak*, a catalog of free-loan film and slide programs produced in a classroom situation and now distributed by Kodak for anyone in schools to view.

Fransecky, Roger B., and Debes, John L. *Visual Literacy: A Way to Learn— A Way to Teach*. Washington, DC: AECT, 1972.

The authors introduce the reader to techniques for using visual literacy in the curriculum. Also included is a short discussion of some of the research done in this area as well as a list of references for further reading.

Gassan, Arnold. *Handbook for Contemporary Photography*. 4th ed. Rochester, NY: Light Impressions, 1977.

This handbook begins with such basics as loading the camera, darkroom development, printing, and enlargement and includes a discussion on storing prints and negatives. The major portion of the book, however, covers advanced controls and special processes for the more serious students of photography.

Getting It on Video/Series I & II. Media Systems, Inc., 3637 East 7800 South, Salt Lake City, UT 84121. n.d.

Each series contains six sound filmstrips that explain how to use video equipment. Individual units contain such information as the video camera, recorder, portable and single camera systems, graphics for television, audio for television, planning a television production, set design, etc. For each filmstrip there is an instructional manual setting for the objectives, teaching strategies, and tests and filmstrip scripts. This company also produces other visual aides helpful in specific equipment operation.

Guide Book: 1973 Edition. Bloomington, IN: National Instructional Television Center, 1973. 32p. (Ed 070 276; Reprint: EDRS).

The National Instructional Television Center (NIT) aims to reduce the time of bringing about educational innovation from the usual 15 years, achieved through traditional means like pre-service education and workshops, to 5 years. Its procedure in doing this is to identify significant ideas and translate them into useful television programs. This booklet describes NIT courses, which consist of television series. The course descriptions are organized by subject matter. For each, the appropriate audience level (which ranges from primary through senior high school as well as teacher training and higher education) is indicated. Also included are an index of courses by grade level and subject matter, a list of NIT prices, procedures, and policies, and descriptions of NIT services and professional publications and films, which deal with instructional television.

Harwood, Don. *Everything You Always Wanted to Know about Video Tape Recording.* 2nd ed. New York: VTR Publishing, 1975.

The book is a technical guide to the use of video tape recorders (vtr) without using technical language. The author explains the vtr's uses, includes charts and instructions for using the separate pieces of equipment, production and editing techniques, and a chapter on preventative maintenance.

Hobson, Andrew, and Hobson, Mark. *Film Animation as a Hobby.* New York: Sterling Publishing, 1975.

The Hobson brothers have written a book that covers all the areas of making animated films. Basic animation techniques, sample clips, and equipment are discussed. The book is especially appropriate for individuals with little to no experience in making animated movies.

Kemp, Jerrold E. *Planning and Producing Audiovisual Materials.* 4th ed. New York: Harper & Row, 1980.

This work proposes to "provide information and experiences that will enable the reader to gain competencies" regarding purposes of using audiovisual materials, reasons for producing them, and planning for their use and production including reasons for the use of a particular medium and instructions for fundamental skills and their application. Each chapter is organized to describe and/or explain a specific area of study. Most are well illustrated with graphic displays of the techniques and intended results.

Langford, Michael. *Visual Aids and Photography in Education; A Visual Aids Manual for Teachers and Learners.* New York: Hastings House, 1973.

The author's twofold purpose for the book is "to show in detail how today's equipment can be used by teachers themselves to make aids, and by learners to expand their knowledge and develop individual creative abilities." Although much of the equipment discussed is somewhat outdated and prices are given as of 1973 (in pounds), the detailed step-by-step methods for making all types of visual aids would be useful for anyone beginning to explore production.

Laybourne, Kit, and Cianciolo, Pauline, eds. *Doing the Media: A Portfolio of Activities, Ideas and Resources.* New rev. ed. New York: McGraw-Hill, 1979.

The editors maintain that *Doing the Media* is "intended to serve as both a practical text in media education courses and as a portfolio of ideas for professional teacher, media specialist, librarian, and others engaged in formal or informal educational activities." The 18 contributors show how nonprint may be integrated into both the elementary and secondary curriculum to make students aware of the influence mass media has over their daily lives. The book provides excellent details and step-by-step procedures for *doing* photography, film, video, sound, and other media. The seventh section deals with the process of designing "an integrated media arts curriculum." The final section of the book is an annotated resources listing of print and nonprint materials, periodicals, organizations, and media distributors.

Linton, Dolores, and Linton, David. *Practical Guide to Classroom Media.* Dayton, OH: Pflaum/Standard, 1971.

The authors have divided the book into two logical divisions: "Laying the Groundwork for Media Involvement" and "Involving Media in the Classroom." Although the illustrations included add very little to the meaning of the text, the value of the book rests in the variety of student activities and projects discussed.

McLaughlin, Frank, ed. *The Mediate Teacher: Seminal Essays on Creative Teaching.* Philadelphia, PA: North American, 1975.

The editor has compiled a collection of essays "about being a special kind of teacher—one who is or intends to be far more attuned and attentive than the average faculty member." A wide variety of topics are presented from "a model for multi-media learning" to "a primer on games" to "films for consciousness raising." The main thrust of the work appears to be for teachers "who recognize that they must be constantly learning and growing if they expect to effectively touch the lives of their students." The book is an essential survival tool for any teacher.

McLuhan, Marshall. *Understanding Media: The Extensions of Man.* New York: McGraw-Hill, 1964.

Although the original publication is now over 16 years old, this book is basic to any secondary collection for students wishing to explore the impact of nonprint on society. The author sets forth his own philosophy and then shows how this opinion is mirrored in the media. McLuhan is widely quoted, and the work itself should continue to be a center for controversy and discussion for years to come.

Media Review. 343 Manville Road, Pleasantville, NY 10570.

This reviewing tool is intended to aid librarians in making nonprint purchases. Monthly supplements offer program summaries and evaluations, new ideas, current funding information, and reviews of professional books.

Media Review Digest. Ann Arbor, MI: Pierian Press, 1973- .

MRD is a basic indexing tool to locate reviews of nonprint appearing in over 200 periodicals. Divisions in the index are according to format: films and videotapes, filmstrips, records and tapes, and miscellaneous media. Bibliographic information is given for each entry.

Miller, Hannah. *Films in the Classroom: A Practical Guide.* Metuchen, NJ: Scarecrow, 1979.
In addition to the coverage given to film in this guide, the author has also included a beginning chapter on nonprint media equipment that covers such information as standards and maintenance of hardware and criteria for judging software selection. There are also six appendices that list details such as organizations helping teachers, students, and librarians understand and use film, professional journals, free and inexpensive sources of films and distributors. The major portion of the text discusses such topics as "film techniques," "types of film," choosing, securing, showing, using, and making films for the classroom.

Minor, Ed, and Frye, Harvey R. *Techniques for Producing Visual Instructional Media.* 2nd ed. New York: McGraw-Hill, 1977.
The book is a step-by-step approach both for the person without graphic skills and the professional seeking new ways to solve problems of visual media production. The directions for each process are described concisely and clearly with accompanying line drawings. There is an extensive glossary of terminology, a bibliography and mediagraphy covering the production area, as well as an address directory of distributors and suppliers of materials.

Minor, Edward. *Handbook for Preparing Visual Media.* 2nd ed. New York: McGraw-Hill, 1978.
The author discusses techniques for illustrating, mounting and laminating materials, lettering and printing, coloring, and producing transparencies for projection and display. Each technique is explained in elaborate detail with specific line drawings accompanying the text for reinforcement.

Morrow, James, and Suid, Murray. *Media & Kids: Real-World Learning in Schools.* Rochelle Park, NJ: Hayden, 1977.
The authors maintain in their preface that the aim of this book is "to bridge the gap between creativity and the curriculum." The introductory essay to the volume titled "Why the medium is not the message" by Morrow sets forth his "vision of the classroom as a place where active production in all media is regarded as a natural way to learn." Two introductory chapters develop a model for multimedia learning and a consideration of pedagogical questions that might influence integration of media production in the classroom. Individual chapters are devoted to design, print, photography, radio, movies, television, and media and people.

National Center for Audio Tapes. University of Colorado, Stadium Building, Boulder, CO 80302. [Most current catalog].
The catalog is compilation of audiotapes for duplication and sale by the National Center for Audio Tapes. The collection is arranged by subject areas with an individual entry description for each tape: title, stock number, producer, broadcast restrictions, grade level, description of contents, and running time. Titles may be ordered either on cassette or reels. Prices include duplication, tape, box with label, mailer, and postage.

National Information Center for Educational Media (NICEM). University of Southern California, University Park, Los Angeles, CA 90007.

NICEM provides indexes to all types of educational media: 16mm films, filmstrips, overhead transparencies, audiotapes, videotapes, records, motion picture cartridges, and slides. The publications are available and frequently updated in hard copy or microfiche. The file is also accessible through the Dialog database information retrieval service for $70.00 per online connect hour.

Oates, S. C. *Audiovisual Equipment Self-Instruction Manual.* 4th ed. Dubuque, IA: W. C. Brown, 1979.

This is one of the most up-to-date compilations of specific models of equipment by type on the market. The manual may be used for self-instruction or for reference when a problem develops during actual operation. Each unit is followed by a quiz to test the user's understanding of the printed text. Single black-and-white illustrations make the instructions easy to follow.

Phillipson, Willard D., and Teach, Beverly, eds. *Educational Film Locator of the Consortium of University Film Centers and R. R. Bowker Company.* 2nd ed. New York: Bowker, 1980.

The tool is "a union list of the titles held by member libraries of the Consortium ... , and a compilation and standardization of their separate catalogs, representing film holdings with their geographic locations." The compilation contains a detailed user's guide that explains the three main approaches to locating information: subject, title and series, and other special features. It should serve as a valuable reference tool for the media specialist who 1) must locate rental sources for 16mm films; 2) is called upon to formulate subject mediagraphies of 16mm titles appropriate for a particular audience; 3) desires to supply the viewer with a descriptive annotation before ordering; 4) needs to verify bibliographic information for cataloging; 5) seeks to identify films that have been produced as a series; or 6) wishes to locate foreign film titles.

Rice, Susan, and Mukerji, Rose, eds. *Children Are Centers for Understanding Media.* Washignton, DC: Association for Childhood Education International, 1973.

This compilation documents the ongoing growth and development of the Center for Understanding Media, which "attempts through its activities to close the gap between the world of school and the world of the new information media." Many of the articles written for this publication were also included in *Doing the Media.* The articles cover a broad spectrum of media production by children of all ages from filmmaking to unusual audiotapes to tap the imagination of the young producers. A unique inclusion is a chapter on flipbooks as a first step to animation. The "Resources for Further Study" is an annotated listing of media, 12 of which have been starred for a "Basic Media Library."

Roach, Helen. *Spoken Records.* 3rd ed. Metuchen, NJ: Scarecrow, 1970.

Although the compilation is ten years old, this is the best tool for selection and evaluation of spoken records across a variety of subject areas. Teachers and media specialists would find this tool useful for establishing a basic spoken record library and for reference to recordings of lectures, speeches, interviews, and authors reading their own works. The author also has a comprehensive analysis of classical and modern literature and plays appropriate for use with preschool through senior high school.

Rosenberg, K. D., and Doskey, J. S. *Media Equipment — A Guide and Dictionary.* Littleton, CO: Libraries Unlimited, 1976.

The book is divided into three major sections: general criteria for equipment selection; specific criteria for individual types of equipment; and a dictionary of terms related to media equipment. The sample checklist forms for individual pieces of equipment would be especially useful when the teacher or media specialist is considering a new purchase.

Rufsvold, Margaret I. *Guides to Educational Media: Films, Filmstrips, Kinescopes, Phonodiscs, Phonotapes, Programmed Instruction Materials, Slides, Transparencies and Videotapes.* 4th ed. Chicago, IL: ALA, 1977.

The purpose of this book as stated by its compiler is "to identify and describe catalogs, indexes, lists, and reviewing services which systematically provide information about educational media." Bibliographies and catalogs included in the guide review all of the formats included in the title. The entries are listed in an author, subject, and title index.

Schillaci, Anthony, and Culkin, John M., eds. *Films Deliver: Teaching Creatively with Film.* New York: Citation Press, 1970.

This compilation of articles is designed "to show interested teachers how to teach creatively through the use of the two most compelling media arts — film and television." The work is divided into three sections; the first is an overview of "What Films Can Do for Teachers and Students" in the curriculum. The other two sections discuss specific areas of the curriculum where films have been used, how to go about selecting appropriate titles, and actual student production activities. Appendices include a filmography of feature and short films, a bibliography of film study, and sample teachers' guides.

Schrank, Jeffrey, ed. *The Seed Catalog; A Guide to Teaching/Learning Materials.* Boston, MA: Beacon, 1974.

The editor, in his introduction to the catalog, proclaims that it is intended "for those in any situation who believe that learning takes place through involvement with a great variety of viewpoints and opinions." Learning, according to the editor, can take place by using both print and nonprint. The contents direct the reader to seek information on publications that "challenge, provoke, and entertain," organizations and little known and unusual periodicals, audiotapes and the alternative radio movement, film, video, games, multimedia, and devices, such as posters, computers, and emotionmeters. The prices of the materials are "comparatively inexpensive rather than a $300 learning package."

Sive, Mary Robinson. *Selecting Instructional Media: A Guide to Audiovisual and Other Instructional Media Lists.* Littleton, CO: Libraries Unlimited, 1978.

The compiler has included 428 published lists of audiovisual and other instructional media appropriate for use with grades K through 12. Each entry contains a complete annotation stating the purpose, grade level, arrangement, subjects, entries, indexes, period covered, revision and updating, media represented, features, and subject terms. The book is intended to aid educators in the selection and purchase of media for curriculum development, for classroom instruction, and for building a collection.

Spirt, D. L. *Library/Media Manual.* New York: H. W. Wilson, 1979.

As the author points out in her introduction, the manual, "which provides instruction on how to get information from a wide variety of communication media, is for students ... who have had little or no instruction in the use of books and nonprint materials." The book is divided into chapters and subdivided into appropriate units with a quiz following each chapter to test for recall. The first chapter is especially helpful, titled "The Library Media Center." In it the author relates "policies, resources and organization" of a media center and "starting the research: using print and nonprint materials." Terminology to be used throughout the text is clearly defined. Chapter two deals with guides to use in accessing print and nonprint. Chapter three is devoted to specific reference books, and chapter four explains the research process: search strategy, taking notes, and formulating a mediagraphy.

"Tell Me What You See." Sound filmstrip. Washington, DC: AECT, 1975.

The program shows how visual literacy is used as a major part of the curriculum in the Milford, Ohio schools. Students learn about visual communications and how to use media to create their own unique message.

Thomas, James L., and Loring, Ruth M., eds. *Motivating Children and Young Adults to Read.* Phoenix, AZ: Oryx Press, 1979.

The book is a compilation of journal articles for teachers faced with the challenge of motivating youngsters to read. One section is devoted to the use of nonprint to entice the nonreader to read.

Thomas, James L. *Nonprint for Students, Teachers and Media Specialists: A Step-by-Step Approach.* Littleton, CO: Libraries Unlimited, 1982.

The author gives specific steps of the procedures for the production of nonprint projects useful in involving students and educators in the learning process. The following chapters are included: transparency lifts and story lamination; slide-tape presentations; filmstrip presentations; super 8mm movie productions; single-camera television programs; and dioramas. Detailed information is given on storyboarding, the materials and hardware needed for each project, and the potential costs.

To Help Them Learn. 16mm film. 21 mins. Color. Washington, DC: AECT & Association of Media Producers, 1977.

The movie shows, through discussion and demonstration, the rationale for using all formats of media to reach the individual student in the learning process. The film is fast-paced and shows teachers interacting with a variety of age groups.

The Video Source Book. Syosset, NY: National Video Clearinghouse, 1979.

Over 15,000 individual pre-recorded video program titles available on videotape or videodisc are included. The compilation is taken from distributors' catalogs and is therefore not a selection tool but a resource guide for locating useful titles in these formats. Titles are listed alphabetically with each carrying full bibliographic data and location information. A category index is supplied divided into broad subject areas. A distributor index is also provided for ordering.

"The Whys and Hows of Student Film Making." Two sound filmstrips. Random House Miller-Brody, 400 Hahn Road, Westminster, MD 21157. 1970.

This program is intended for use by teachers who wish to gain insight into the movie making process as it relates to classroom education and development of visual literacy skills. A paperback book on the basic techniques of filmmaking is also included.

Williams, Frank E. *Media Resource Book: The Total Creativity Program for Individualizing and Humanizing the Learning Process.* Volume 4. Englewood Cliffs, NJ: Educational Technology Publications, 1972. 77p. (ED 070 244 or available from: Educational Technology Publications, 140 Sylvan Ave., Englewood Cliffs, NJ 07632).

Books and films that are directly useful in producing the eight thinking-feeling processes of the cognitive-affective interaction (CAI) model on which this complete program is based are listed. (See ED 010 276 for the rationale for and discussion of this model.) Ninety-two books appropriate to the pupil processes and teaching strategies of the CAI model are listed along with suggested grade level and a short annotation. Seventy films are alphabetized by title. The films are also classified by pupil process and teaching strategy. Eighteen curriculum programs or materials designed to develop certain thinking-feeling processes are listed alphabetically by title of program or material.

Wiman, Raymond. *Instructional Materials; An Illustrated Handbook of Ideas, Skills, and Techniques for Producing and Using Audiovisual Materials.* Worthington, OH: C. A. Jones, 1972.

A how-to-do-it information manual for teachers and media specialists about photography, transparency production, lettering, drawing, bulletin boards, dry mounting, and operation of equipment. Simple line drawings make the handbook practical and easy to follow.

Wittich, W. A., and Schuller, C. F. *Instructional Technology: Its Nature and Use.* 5th ed. New York: Harper & Row, 1973.

The textbook is intended as a bridge between theory and practice in showing how media and technology might be used "in actual teaching involving a variety of instructional strategies." The authors show how instructional technology is used to improve learning and how essential the teacher is to the effective use of this technology. The majority of the work deals with individual media as they relate to the learning process. *A Student Production Guide* has been developed to reinforce the main text.

APPENDIX I:
A SELECTIVE LISTING OF
PERIODICALS EVALUATING NONPRINT

The following periodicals useful for the school curriculum include a wide variety of media—both print and nonprint. In order to see if a specific title meets a need in the selection of nonprint, the reader is encouraged to write to the individual publisher for a sample copy and price schedule.

AMP REPORTS

Association of Media Producers, Inc.
Suite 515
1707 L Street, NW
Washington, DC 20036

AV GUIDE

Educational Screen, Inc.
434 S. Wabash Avenue
Chicago, IL 60605

AMERICAN BIOLOGY TEACHER

National Association of Biology Teachers
11250 Roger Bacon Drive
Reston, VA 22090

AMERICAN CINEMATOGRAPHER

American Society of Cinematographers
1782 N. Orange Drive
Hollywood, CA 90028

AMERICAN FILM

American Film Institute
John F. Kennedy Center for the
   Performing Arts
Washington, DC 20566

AMERICAN RECORD GUIDE

ARG Publishing, Inc.
One Windsor Place
Melville, NY 11746

THE ANIMATOR

Northwest Film Study Center
Northland Art Museum
Southwest Park & Madison
Portland, OR 97205

ARTS & ACTIVITIES

Publishers' Development Corporation
Camino de la Reina, Suite 200
San Diego, CA 92108

ATHLETIC JOURNAL

Athletic Journal Publishing Company
1719 Howard Street
Evanston, IL 60202

AUDIO

North American Publishing Company
401 N. Broad Street
Philadelphia, PA 19108

AUDIO-VISUAL COMMUNICATIONS

United Business Publications, Inc.
475 Park Avenue South
New York, NY 10016

AUDIO-VISUAL JOURNAL

Audio-Visual Library Service
University of Minnesota
3300 University Avenue, SE
Minneapolis, MN 55414

AUDIO VISUAL NEWS BRIEFS

Association of National Advertisers
155 E. 44th Street
New York, NY 10017

BETTER RADIO & TELEVISION

National Association for Better
 Broadcasting
Box 43640
Los Angeles, CA 90043

BOOKLIST

American Library Association
50 E. Huron Street
Chicago, IL 60611

CATHOLIC FILM NEWSLETTER

Office for Film & Broadcasting
U.S. Catholic Conference
1011 First Avenue, Suite 1300
New York, NY 10022

THE CLEARINGHOUSE

Helen Dwight Reid Educational
 Foundation
4000 Albermarle Street, NW
Washington, DC 20016

CURRENT INDEX TO JOURNALS
 IN EDUCATION

Oryx Press
2214 North Central at Encanto
Phoenix, AZ 85004

CURRICULUM PRODUCT REVIEW

McGraw-Hill, Inc.
230 W. Monroe Street
Suite 1100
Chicago, IL 60606

EDUCATIONAL & INDUSTRIAL
 TELEVISION

C. S. Tepfer Publishing Company, Inc.
51 Sugar Hollow Road
Danbury, CT 06810

EDUCATIONAL DIGEST

Maclean Hunter Ltd.
481 University Avenue
Toronto, Ontario M5W 1A7, Canada

EDUCATIONAL SCREEN &
AUDIOVISUAL GUIDE

Educational Screen, Inc.
434 S. Wabash Avenue
Chicago, IL 60605

EDUCATIONAL TECHNOLOGY

Educational Technology Publications, Inc.
140 Sylvan Avenue
Englewood Cliffs, NJ 07632

EFLA EVALUATIONS

Educational Film Library Association, Inc.
43 W. 61st Street
New York, NY 10023

ELEMENTARY ENGLISH

National Council of Teachers of English
1111 Kenyon Road
Urbana, IL 61801

ELEMENTARY SCHOOL JOURNAL

University of Chicago Press
5835 Kimbark Avenue
Chicago, IL 60637

ENGLISH JOURNAL

National Council of Teachers of English
1111 Kenyon Road
Urbana, IL 61801

EPIEgram: MATERIALS

The Educational Products Information
Exchange (EPIE) Institute
475 Riverside Drive
New York, NY 10027

ETV NEWSLETTER

C. S. Tepfer Publishing Company, Inc.
607 Main Street
Ridgefield, CT 06877

EXCEPTIONAL CHILDREN

The Council for Exceptional Children
1920 Association Drive
Reston, VA 22091

FILM COMMENT

The Film Society of Lincoln Center
1865 Broadway
New York, NY 10023

FILM LIBRARY QUARTERLY

Film Library Information Council
Box 348
Radio City Station
New York, NY 10019

FILM NEWS

Film News Company
250 W. 57th Street, Suite 2202
New York, NY 10019

FILM QUARTERLY

University of California Press
Berkeley, CA 94720

G P NEWSLETTER

Great Plains National Instructional
Television Library
Box 80669
Lincoln, NE 68501

GRADE TEACHER

Macmillan Professional Magazines, Inc.
1 Fawcett Place
Greenwich, CT 06830

HIGH FIDELITY MAGAZINE

ABC Leisure Magazine, Inc.
The Publishing House
Great Barrington, MA 01230

HORN BOOK MAGAZINE

Horn Book, Inc.
Park Square Building
31st Street & James Avenue
Boston, MA 02116

INDUSTRIAL EDUCATION

Macmillan Professional Magazines, Inc.
1 Fawcett Place
Greenwich, CT 06830

INSTRUCTIONAL INNOVATOR

Association for Educational
  Communications and Technology
1126 16th Street, NW
Washington, DC 20036

INSTRUCTOR

The Instructor Publications, Inc.
Seven Bank Street
Dansville, NY 14437

INTERNATIONAL JOURNAL OF
INSTRUCTIONAL MEDIA

Baywood Publishing Company
120 Marine Street
Farmingdale, NY 11735

JOURNAL OF EDUCATIONAL
TECHNOLOGY SYSTEMS

Baywood Publishing Company
120 Marine Street
Farmingdale, NY 11735

JOURNAL OF GEOGRAPHY

National Council for Geographic
  Education
Department of Geography
Western Illinois University
Macomb, IL 61455

JOURNAL OF HEALTH, PHYSICAL
EDUCATION, RECREATION

American Association for Health,
  Physical Education, and Recreation
1201 16th Street, NW
Washington, DC 20036

JOURNAL OF LEARNING
DISABILITIES

Professional Press, Inc.
101 E. Ontario Street
Chicago, IL 60611

JOURNAL OF POPULAR FILM
& TELEVISION

Center for Popular Culture
Bowling Green State University
Bowling Green, OH 43403

K-eight

134 North 13th Street
Philadelphia, PA 19107

K-3 BULLETIN OF TEACHING IDEAS
& MATERIALS

Parker Publishing Company
Prentice-Hall
West Nyack, NY 10994

LANDERS FILM REVIEWS

Landers Associates
Box 69760
Los Angeles, CA 90069

LANGUAGE ARTS

National Council of Teachers of English
1111 Kenyon Road
Urbana, IL 61801

LEARNING

Education Today Company, Inc.
530 University Avenue
Palo Alto, CA 94301

LIBRARY TECHNOLOGY REPORTS

American Library Association
50 E. Huron Street
Chicago, Il 60611

LISTENING POST	Bro-Dart, Inc. 1236 S. Hatcher City of Industry, CA 91748
LJ/SLJ HOTLINE	R. R. Bowker Company 1180 Avenue of the Americas New York, NY 10036
MAN/SOCIETY/TECHNOLOGY: A JOURNAL OF INDUSTRIAL EDUCATION	American Industrial Arts Association, Inc. 1201 16th Street, NW Washington, DC 20036
MATHEMATICS TEACHER	National Council of Teachers of Mathematics 1906 Association Drive Reston, VA 22091
MEDIA & METHODS	North American Publishing Company 401 Broad Street Philadelphia, PA 19108
MEDIA DIGEST	National Film & Video Center 4321 Sykesville Road Finksburg, MD 21048
MEDIA MIX	Claretian Publications 221 W. Madison Chicago, IL 60606
MODERN LANGUAGE JOURNAL	National Federation of Modern Language Teachers Associations 30A McKenna Building University of Colorado Boulder, CO 80309
NOTES	Music Library Association, Inc. 343 S. Main Street, Room 205 Ann Arbor, MI 48108
PREVIEWS	R. R. Bowker Company 1180 Avenue of the Americas New York, NY 10036
PTST	Prime Time School Television 120 South LaSalle Street Chicago, IL 60603
PUBLIC TELECOMMUNICATIONS REVIEW	National Association of Educational Broadcasters 1346 Connecticut Avenue, NW Washington, DC 20036
RADICAL SOFTWARE/CHANGING CHANNELS	Gordon & Breach Science Publishers Ltd. 42 William IV Street London WC2, England
RECORDED VISUAL INSTRUCTION	Great Plains National Instructional Television Library (GPN) Box 80669 Lincoln, NE 68501

RELIGION TEACHER'S JOURNAL

Twenty Third Publications
Box 180
West Mystic, CT 06388

RESOURCES IN EDUCATION

Educational Resources Information Center
National Institute of Education
Washington, DC 20208

ROCKINGCHAIR

Cupola Productions
Box 27-K
Philadelphia, PA 19105

SCHOOL ARTS MAGAZINE

Davis Publishing, Inc.
Printers Building
50 Portland Street
Worcester, MA 01608

SCHOOL LIBRARY JOURNAL

R. R. Bowker Company
1180 Avenue of the Americas
New York, NY 10036

SCHOOL MEDIA QUARTERLY

American Library Association
50 E. Huron Street
Chicago, IL 60611

SCHOOL PRODUCT NEWS

Industrial Publishing Company
614 Superior W.
Cleveland, OH 44113

SCIENCE ACTIVITIES

HELDREF Publications
4000 Albemarle Street, NW, Suite 510
Washington, DC 20016

SCIENCE BOOKS & FILMS

American Association for the
   Advancement of Science
1776 Massachusetts Avenue, NW
Washington, DC 20036

SCIENCE TEACHER

National Science Teachers Association
1742 Connecticut Avenue, NW
Washington, DC 20009

SIGHTLINES

Educational Film Library Association
43 W. 61st Street
New York, NY 10023

SNEAK PREVIEW, THE MEDIA
DIGEST

National Educational Film Center
Finksburg, MD 21048

SOCIAL EDUCATION

National Council for the Social Studies
1515 Wilson Boulevard
Arlington, VA 22209

SOCIAL STUDIES

McKinley Publishing Company
112 S. New Broadway
Brooklawn, NJ 08030

STEREO REVIEW

Ziff-Davis Publishing Company
One Park Avenue
New York, NY 10016

SUPER-8 FILMMAKER	PMS Publishing Company, Inc. 3161 Fillmore Street San Francisco, CA 94123
TEACHER MAGAZINE	Macmillan Professional Magazines, Inc. 77 Bedford Street Stamford, CT 06901
TEACHING EXCEPTIONAL CHILDREN	Council for Exceptional Children 1920 Association Drive Reston, VA 22091
TODAY'S CATHOLIC TEACHER	Peter Li, Inc. 2451 E. River Road Dayton, OH 45439
TODAY'S EDUCATION	Journal of the National Education Association 1201 16th Street, NW Washington, DC 20036
TOP OF THE NEWS	American Library Association 50 E. Huron Street Chicago, IL 60611
TRAINING FILM PROFILES	Olympic Media Information 71 W. 23rd Street New York, NY 10010
TV GUIDE	TV Guide Box 400 Radnor, PA 19088
VIDEO NEWS	Phillips Publishing, Inc. 8401 Connecticut Avenue, Suite 707 Washington, DC 20015

APPENDIX II:
ORGANIZATIONS CONCERNED
WITH NONPRINT

Name & Address	Publication(s)
Academy for Educational Development, Inc. 680 Fifth Avenue New York, NY 10019	
Action for Children's Television (ACT) 46 Austin Street Newtonville, MA 02160	NEWSLETTER
Agency for Instructional Television Box A Bloomington, IN 47401	AIT NEWSLETTER
American Association of Museums 1055 Thomas Jefferson Street, NW Washington, DC 20007	MUSEUM NEWS
American Association of School Administrators 1801 N. Moore Street Arlington, VA 22209	THE SCHOOL ADMINISTRATOR
American Association of School Librarians (AASL) 50 E. Huron Street Chicago, IL 60611	SCHOOL MEDIA QUARTERLY
The American Film Institute The John F. Kennedy Center for the Performing Arts Washington, DC 20566	AMERICAN FILM
American Foundation for the Blind, Inc. 15 W. 16th Street New York, NY 10011	AFB NEWSLETTER; JOURNAL OF VISUAL IMPAIRMENT & BLINDNESS; WASHINGTON REPORT
American Library Association (ALA) 50 E. Huron Street Chicago, IL 60611	AMERICAN LIBRARIES; BOOKLIST; TOP OF THE NEWS
American Science Film Association 3624 Market Street Philadelphia, PA 19104	ASFA NOTES

American Theatre Association
1000 Vermont Avenue, NW
Washington, DC 20005

SECONDARY SCHOOL THEATRE
JOURNAL; CHILDREN'S THEATRE
REVIEW

Association for Childhood Education
International
3615 Wisconsin Avenue, NW
Washington, DC 20016

CHILDHOOD EDUCATION

Association for Educational
Communications and Technology
(AECT)
1126 16th Street, NW
Washington, DC 20036

INSTRUCTIONAL INNOVATOR

Association for Supervision and
Curriculum Development
1701 K Street, NW, Suite 1100
Washington, DC 20006

EDUCATIONAL LEADERSHIP

Association of Media Producers
1707 L Street, NW, Suite 515
Washington, DC 20006

AMP REPORTS

Broadcasting Foundation of America
52 Vanderbilt Avenue, Suite 1810
New York, NY 10017

Carnegie Council on Children
1619 Broadway
New York, NY 10019

Catholic Library Association
461 W. Lancaster Avenue
Haverford, PA 19041

CATHOLIC LIBRARY WORLD

Center for Understanding Media
66 Fifth Avenue
New York, NY 10014

Children's Television Workshop (CTM)
One Lincoln Plaza
New York, NY 10023

Consortium of University Film Centers
c/o Visual Aids Service
University of Illinois
Champaign, IL 61820

EDUCATIONAL FILM LOCATOR

Educational Film Library Association,
Inc.
43 W. 61st Street
New York, NY 10023

SIGHTLINES

Educational Resources Information
Center (ERIC)
National Institute of Education
Washington, DC 20208

RESOURCES IN EDUCATION;
CURRENT INDEX TO JOURNALS
IN EDUCATION; THESAURUS OF
ERIC DESCRIPTORS; RESOURCES
IN INFORMATION EDUCATION

Educational Products Information
  Exchange Institute (EPIE)
475 Riverside Drive
New York, NY 10027

EPIEgram; EQUIPMENT

Film Library Information Council
Box 348
Radio City Station
New York, NY 10019

FILM LIBRARY QUARTERLY

Foundation to Improve Television
50 Congress Street
Boston, MA 02109

Foxfire Fund
Route 1
Rabun Gap, GA 30568

FOXFIRE

Industrial Audio-Visual Association
Box 656
Downtown Station
Chicago, IL 60690

International Quorum of Motion Picture
  Producers (IQ)
Box 395
Oakton, VA 22124

QUORUM QUOTES

International Tape Exchange
834 Ruddiman Avenue
North Muskegon, MI 49445

PUPILS SPEAK TO PUPILS AROUND
  THE WORLD

Media Action Research Center (MARC)
475 Riverside Drive, Suite 1370
New York, NY 10027

Media Center for Children
43 W. 61st Street
New York, NY 10023

YOUNG VIEWERS

The Modern Language Association of
  America
62 Fifth Avenue
New York, NY 10011

PMLA; MLA NEWSLETTER

Music Educators National Conference
1902 Association Drive
Reston, VA 22091

MUSIC EDUCATORS JOURNAL

National Association of Elementary
  School Principals
1801 N. Moore Street
Arlington, VA 22209

THE NATIONAL ELEMENTARY
  PRINCIPAL

National Audio-Visual Association
  (NAVA)
3150 Spring Street
Fairfax, VA 22031

AUDIO-VISUAL EQUIPMENT
  DIRECTORY; A-V CONNECTION;
  THE GUIDE TO FEDERAL FUNDS
  FOR AUDIO-VISUAL PROGRAMS

National Council of Teachers of English
1111 Kenyon Road
Urbana, IL 61801

LANGUAGE ARTS; ENGLISH
JOURNAL

National Film Board of Canada
Box 6100
Montreal, Quebec H3C 3H5, Canada

National Public Radio
2025 M Street, NW
Washington, DC 20036

Prime Time School Television (PTST)
120 S. LaSalle Street
Chicago, IL 60603

Society for Applied Learning Technology
50 Culpeper Street
Warrenton, VA 22186

JOURNAL OF EDUCATIONAL
TECHNOLOGY SYSTEMS

Workshop for Learning Things
5 Bridge Street
Watertown, MA 02172

CATALOG

Youth Film Distribution Center
43 W. 16th Street
New York, NY 10011

CATALOG

APPENDIX III:
PRODUCERS OF NONPRINT MATERIALS

Most of the producers included in this listing supply a wide variety of media. Those usually limited to one medium can be easily located by their descriptive titles; for example, "color slides" or "films." Also, the subject areas indicated are those appropriate for this compilation and audience. Some of the producers do provide materials in other areas and for undergraduate and professional programs.

Grade range abbreviations used in the listing:

J   - Junior High School Media
S   - Senior High School Media
J-S - Junior & Senior High School Media

Name & Address	Grade Range	the arts	education	home economics	humanities	industrial/vocational ed	languages	library science/media	mathematics	music/performing arts	physical education/sports	science	social sciences
ABC Media Concepts 1330 Avenue of the Americas New York, NY 10019	J-S	x	x	x	x	x				x	x	x	x
ABT Publications 55 Wheeler Street Cambridge, MA 02138	J-S			x	x		x	x					x
Academy Films Inc Box 38753 Hollywood, CA 90038	J-S	x			x						x	x	x
Acorn Films Inc 33 Union Square W. New York, NY 10003	J-S		x								x	x	
Advance Process Supply Company 400 N. Noble Street Chicago, IL 60622	J-S	x											
Advanced Systems Inc 1601 Tonne Road Elk Grove Village, IL 60007	S						x		x			x	x
Aero Products Research Inc 11201 Hindry Avenue Los Angeles, CA 90045	J-S										x		
Aetna Life & Casualty 151 Farmington Avenue Hartford, CT 06156	J-S		x										x
AEVAC Inc 1500 Park Avenue South Plainfield, NJ 07080	J-S				x								x
Afro Audio-Visual Company 141 Spencer Street Dorchester, MA 02124	J-S												x
Afro-Am Inc 910 S. Michigan Avenue Chicago, IL 60605	J-S												x

Name & Address	Grade Range	the arts	education	home economics	humanities	industrial/vocational ed	languages	library science/media	mathematics	music/performing arts	physical education/sports	science	social sciences
Agency for Instructional Television Box A, 1111 W. 17th Street Bloomington, IN 47401	J-S	x	x		x	x		x	x			x	x
Alemann Films 102110 San Pascual Avenue Los Angeles, CA 90042	J-S	x			x								
Allyn & Bacon Inc 470 Atlantic Avenue Boston, MA 02210	J-S		x	x	x	x		x				x	x
Altair Productions Box 16008 San Francisco, CA 94116	S									x		x	
Aluminum Association 818 Connecticut Avenue, NW Washington, DC 20006	J-S											x	
American Book Company 135 W. 50th Street New York, NY 10020	J-S				x				x				
American Educational Films 132 Lasky Drive Beverly Hills, CA 90212	J-S	x	x	x	x				x	x		x	x
American Institute of Architects 1735 New York Avenue, NW Washington, DC 20006	S	x											x
American Library Color Slide Co Inc Box 5810, Grand Central Station New York, NY 10017	J-S	x										x	
American Map Co Inc 1926 Broadway New York, NY 10023	J-S	x			x		x					x	x
American Meteorite Laboratory Box 2098 Denver, CO 80201	S											x	

Name & Address	Grade Range	the arts	education	home economics	humanities	industrial/vocational ed	languages	library science/media	mathematics	music/performing arts	physical education/sports	science	social sciences
American Museum of Natural History Library-Photographic Collection Central Park W. at 79th Street New York, NY 10024	J-S	x		x						x		x	x
Paul S Amidon & Assoc Inc 1966 Benson Avenue St. Paul, MN 55116	J-S		x						x			x	x
Ken Anderson Films Inc Box 618 1520 E. Winona Street Winona Lake Warsaw, IN 46590	J-S				x						x		
Appalshop Inc Box 743, 118 Main Street Whitesburg, KY 41858	J-S	x	x	x	x					x		x	x
Applause Productions Inc 85 Longview Road Port Washington, NY 11050	J-S					x				x		x	
Aptos Film Productions Inc Box 1638 Thomasville, GA 31792	J-S											x	
Architectural Color Slides 187 Grant Street Lexington, MA 02173	J-S	x										x	
Ralph Arlyck Films 79 Raymond Avenue Poughkeepsie, NY 12601	S	x	x		x					x	x	x	
Aspect IV Educational Films Sub of Business Films, Inc 41 Riverside Avenue Westport, CT 06880	J-S		x									x	
Associated Educational Materials Company 14 Glenwood Avenue, Box 2087 Raleigh, NC 27602	J		x	x	x				x				

Name & Address	Grade Range	the arts	education	home economics	humanities	industrial/vocational ed	languages	library science/media	mathematics	music/performing arts	physical education/sports	science	social sciences
The Athletic Institute Inc 200 Castlewood Drive North Palm Beach, FL 33408	J-S									x	x		
Atlantis Productions Inc 850 Thousand Oaks Boulevard Thousand Oaks, CA 91360	J-S		x	x	x								x
Audio Book Company 14937 Ventura Boulevard Sherman Oaks, CA 91403	J-S		x										
Audio Visual Enterprises 911 Laguna Road Pasadena, CA 91105	J	x										x	x
Audio Visual Narrative Arts Inc 29 Marble Avenue Pleasantville, NY 10570	J-S	x	x	x	x							x	x
Audio-Visual School Service 155 W. 72nd Street New York, NY 10023	J-S		x	x								x	x
Leland Auslender Films 6036 Comey Avenue Los Angeles, CA 90034	J-S	x	x		x						x		
AV-ED Films 910 N. Citrus Avenue Hollywood, CA 90038	J-S	x	x	x	x	x					x	x	x
Lem Bailey Productions 910 N. Citrus Avenue Los Angeles, CA 90038	J-S	x	x		x							x	x
Bandera Enterprises Inc Box 1107 Studio City, CA 91604	S		x	x							x	x	x
Barr Films 3490 E. Foothill Boulevard Pasadena, CA 91107	J-S	x	x	x	x				x		x	x	x

Name & Address	Grade Range	the arts	education	home economics	humanities	industrial/vocational ed	languages	library science/media	mathematics	music/performing arts	physical education/sports	science	social sciences
Bee Cross-Media Inc 36 Dogwood Glen Rochester, NY 14625	J-S	x											
Benefic Press 10300 W. Roosevelt Road Westchester, IL 60153	J											x	x
Bergwall Productions Inc 839 Stewart Avenue Garden City, NY 11530	J-S	x	x	x						x	x		
Berklee Press Publications 1265 Boylston Street Boston, MA 02164	J-S									x			
Channing L Bete Co Inc 45 Federal Street Greenfield, MA 01301	J-S		x	x								x	x
Bilingual Educational Services Inc 1603 Hope Street South Pasadena, CA 91030	J-S						x					x	x
Biological Sciences Curriculum Study Box 930 Boulder, CO 80306	J-S											x	
Biomedical Communications University of Nebraska Medical Center 42 & Dewey Omaha, NE 68105	S											x	
Bill Boal Productions Inc 100 Fifth Avenue New York, NY 10011	J-S	x		x						x	x	x	x
BNA Communications Inc 9401 Decoverly Hall Road Rockville, MD 20850	S		x										x

Name & Address	Grade Range	the arts	education	home economics	humanities	industrial/vocational ed	languages	library science/media	mathematics	music/performing arts	physical education/sports	science	social sciences
Board of Jewish Education Inc 426 W. 58th Street New York, NY 10019	J-S	x	x				x			x			
Borden Productions Inc Box 520 Great Meadows Road Concord, MA 01742	J-S		x								x	x	x
Borg-Warner Educational Systems Sub of Borg-Warner Corp 600 W. University Drive Arlington Heights, IL 60004	J						x	x					
Bortnick Film Productions Ltd 465 Kingston Crescent Winnipeg, Manitoba R2M OV1, Canada	J-S				x								x
Don Bosco Films & Filmstrips 148 Main Street Box T New Rochelle, NY 10802	J-S	x	x									x	x
Stephen Bosustow Productions 1649 11th Street Santa Monica, CA 90404	J-S		x		x			x					x
Thomas Bouchard Stony Brook Road West Brewster, MA 02631	S	x								x			
Bowmar/Noble Publishers Inc 4563 Colorado Boulevard Los Angeles, CA 90039	J		x						x				x
Robert J Brady Company Routes 450 & 197 Bowie, MD 20715	J-S	x	x	x									x
Brazos Films 10341 San Pablo Avenue El Cerrito, CA 94530	J-S				x		x			x			

Name & Address	Grade Range	the arts	education	home economics	humanities	industrial/vocational ed	languages	library science/media	mathematics	music/performing arts	physical education/sports	science	social sciences
Brigham Young University W-Stad Provo, UT 84602	J-S		x	x	x								x
Broadcasting Foundation of America Suite 1810 52 Vanderbilt Avenue New York, NY 10017	J-S	x	x		x							x	x
William Brose Productions Inc 10850 Riverside Drive North Hollywood, CA 91603	S		x	x									x
The E C Brown Foundation 710 S.W. Second Avenue Portland, OR 97204	J-S		x										x
Billy Budd Films Inc 235 E. 57th Street New York, NY 10022	J-S		x										
Budek Films & Slides 73 Pelham Street Newport, RI 02840	J-S	x	x										
Bullfrog Films Inc Oley, PA 19547	J-S	x	x	x								x	x
Bureau of Jewish Education 6505 Wilshire Boulevard Los Angeles, CA 90048	J-S	x	x										
Butterick Publishing 708 Third Avenue New York, NY 10017	J-S		x	x									x
Caedmon 1995 Broadway New York, NY 10023	J-S	x	x		x		x			x			x
Campbell Films Inc Cory Hill Saxtons River, VT 05154	S	x	x										

Name & Address	Grade Range	the arts	education	home economics	humanities	industrial/vocational ed	languages	library science/media	mathematics	music/performing arts	physical education/sports	science	social sciences
Capitol Records Inc 1750 N. Vine Street Hollywood, CA 90028	J-S	x	x	x	x	x			x	x	x	x	x
Carolina Biological Supply Co 2700 York Road Burlington, NC 27215	J-S		x									x	x
Cavalcade Productions Inc Box 801 Wheaton, IL 60187	J-S											x	x
Cellar Door Cinema Drawer P Osterville, MA 02655	J-S	x											
Center for Cassette Studies Inc 8110 Webb Avenue North Hollywood, CA 91605	J-S	x	x	x	x				x		x	x	x
The Center for Humanities Inc Communications Park Box 100 White Plains, NY 10602	J-S	x	x	x	x				x		x	x	x
Center for Southern Folklore 1216 Peabody Box 4081 Memphis, TN 38104	J-S	x			x					x			x
Centron Educational Films 1621 W. Ninth Lawrence, KS 66044	J-S	x	x	x	x							x	x
Cereal Institute Inc 1111 Plaza Drive Schaumburg, IL 60195	J-S		x	x									
Chamber of Commerce of the US 1615 H Street, NW Washington, DC 20062	J-S												x
Children's Classics on Tape 6722 Bostwick Drive Springfield, VA 22151	J												x

Name & Address	Grade Range	the arts	education	home economics	humanities	industrial/vocational ed	languages	library science/media	mathematics	music/performing arts	physical education/sports	science	social sciences
Children's Press 1224 W. Van Buren Chicago, IL 60607	J		x				x			x	x	x	x
Chilton Book Company 201 King of Prussia Road Radnor, PA 19089	S					x						x	
Chimera Foundation for Dance Inc 33 E. 18th Street New York, NY 10003	S	x								x			
Churchill Films 662 N. Robertson Boulevard Los Angeles, CA 90069	J-S	x	x	x				x		x	x	x	x
Cinematic Concepts Corporation 1761 Broadway San Francisco, CA 94109	J-S		x										x
Cine'-Pic Hawaii 1847 Pacific Heights Road Honolulu, HI 96813	J-S	x	x							x	x	x	x
Civic Education Service 5420 27th Street, NW Washington, DC 20015	J-S												x
William Claiborne 33 Union Square W. New York, NY 10003	J-S	x	x		x		x		x			x	x
Clarke Irwin & Co Ltd 791 St. Clair Avenue W. Toronto, Ontario M6C 1B8, Canada	J-S		x				x						x
Clarus Music Ltd 340 Bellevue Avenue Yonkers, NY 10703	J-S	x	x		x					x			x
Classroom World Productions Box 28166 Raleigh, NC 27611	J-S	x	x	x	x		x		x	x	x	x	x

Name & Address	Grade Range	the arts	education	home economics	humanities	industrial/vocational ed	languages	library science/media	mathematics	music/performing arts	physical education/sports	science	social sciences
Colonial Films 4315 ND Expressway Atlanta, GA 30341	J-S		x										
Colonial Williamsburg Foundation AV Distribution Section, Box C Williamsburg, VA 23185	J-S	x								x		x	x
Colorado Mining Association 1515 Cleveland Place Denver, CO 80202	J		x									x	
Columbia Special Products 51 W. 52nd Street New York, NY 10019	J-S		x		x	x			x			x	x
Communacad, The Communications Academy Box 541 Wilton, CT 06897	J-S		x										
Communications Group West 6606 Sunset Boulevard Hollywood, CA 90028	J-S		x	x						x		x	x
Community Development Foundation 48 Wilton Road Westport, CT 06880	S				x	x							x
Comprenetics Inc 340 N. Camden Drive Beverly Hills, CA 90210	J-S	x	x	x									
C G Conn Ltd 616 Enterprise Drive Oak Brook, IL 60521	J-S									x			
Consumers Union 256 Washington Street Mt. Vernon, NY 10550	J-S												x
Contempo Communications Inc 1841 Broadway New York, NY 10023	S	x	x		x					x	x		

Name & Address	Grade Range	the arts	education	home economics	humanities	industrial/vocational ed	languages	library science/media	mathematics	music/performing arts	physical education/sports	science	social sciences
David C Cook Publishing Co Public & Private School Division 850 N. Grove Street Elgin, IL 60120	J		x									x	x
Copymotion 1600 Broadway, Box 5173 New York, NY 10017	J	x				x			x	x			
Cornell Laboratory of Ornithology 159 Sapsucker Woods Road Ithaca, NY 14853	J-S											x	
Coronet Films 65 E. South Water Street Chicago, IL 60601	J-S	x	x	x	x		x		x	x		x	x
Counselor Films Inc 146 Montgomery Avenue Bala Cynwyd, PA 19004	J-S	x	x		x					x		x	x
Counterpoint Films 14622 Lanark Street Panorama City, CA 91402	J-S		x		x								x
Thomas Craven Corporation 316 E. 53rd Street New York, NY 10022	S											x	
Creative Learning Inc 38 Nayatt Road Barrington, RI 02806	J	x	x						x			x	x
Creative Visuals Division/Gamco Industries Inc Box 1911 Big Spring, TX 79720	J-S		x	x	x		x		x				x
CRM/McGraw-Hill Films Del Mar, CA 92014	S		x		x							x	x
Crystal Productions 107 Pacific Avenue, Box 11480 Aspen, CO 81611	J-S	x	x	x							x	x	x

Name & Address	Grade Range	the arts	education	home economics	humanities	industrial/vocational ed	languages	library science/media	mathematics	music/performing arts	physical education/sports	science	social sciences
James Culp Productions 917C Santa Clara Avenue Alameda, CA 94501	S	x	x		x					x			x
Current Affairs/Young World 24 Danbury Road Wilton, CT 06897	J-S	x	x	x	x	x					x	x	x
Cypress Publishing Corporation 1763 Gardena Avenue Glendale, CA 91204	J-S		x	x						x		x	x
Dana Productions 6249 Babcock Avenue North Hollywood, CA 91606	J-S	x	x		x					x			x
Dan-Glenn Productions Box 8307 Universal City, CA 91608	J-S		x		x							x	x
Daughters of St. Paul 50 St. Paul's Avenue Boxton, MA 02130	J-S												x
Davco Publishers 8154 Ridgeway Skokie, IL 60076	J-S												x
Tom Davenport Films Pearlsone, Delaplane, VA 22025	J-S	x			x					x			x
DCA Educational Products 424 Valley Road Warrington, PA 18976	J-S	x	x	x									
Walter de Gruyter Inc 200 Saw Mill River Road Hawthorne, NY 10532	S											x	
Delisle Productions Ltd 40 St. Clair Avenue W. Toronto, Ontario, Canada	S											x	
Murl Deusing Film Productions 1401 W. Hwy 50 Lot 163 Clermont, FL 32711	J-S											x	x

Name & Address	Grade Range	the arts	education	home economics	humanities	industrial/vocational ed	languages	library science/media	mathematics	music/performing arts	physical education/sports	science	social sciences
Dimension Pictures 9000 W. Sunset Boulevard Los Angeles, CA 90069	J-S		x		x					x	x	x	x
Discovery Productions 151 E. 50th Street New York, NY 10022	J-S	x	x		x					x	x	x	x
Walt Disney Educational Media Co 500 S. Buena Vista Street Burbank, CA 91521	J-S		x		x	x		x				x	x
Docent Corporation 430 Manville Road Pleasantville, NY 10570	J-S	x	x		x					x			
Document Associates Inc 211 E. 43rd Street New York, NY 10017	S	x	x	x						x	x	x	x
Documentaries for Learning 58 Fenwood Road Boston, MA 02115	S		x							x			x
Documentary Educational Resources Inc 24 Dane Street Somerville, MA 02143	S				x					x			x
Donars Productions 407 N. Lincoln Avenue Loveland, CO 80537	J-S	x	x	x	x	x						x	x
Kevin Donovan Films Box 309 Glastonbury, CT 06033	J-S					x						x	x
Double Sixteen Company Box 1616 Wheaton, IL 60187	J-S			x									
Dover Publications Inc 180 Varick Street New York, NY 10014	S					x				x			

Name & Address	Grade Range	the arts	education	home economics	humanities	industrial/vocational ed	languages	library science/media	mathematics	music/performing arts	physical education/sports	science	social sciences
Edplan Corporation Box 4361 Grand Central Station New York, NY 10017	J-S	x	x										x
Educational Activities Inc Box 392 Freeport, NY 11520	J-S		x	x	x				x	x		x	x
Educational Audio Visual Inc Pleasantville, NY 10570	J-S	x	x	x	x	x		x	x	x	x	x	x
Educational Communication Assoc 822 National Press Building Washington, DC 20045	J-S	x	x		x	x				x			x
Educational Design Inc 47 W. 13th Street New York, NY 10011	J-S		x	x	x	x						x	x
Educational Development Corporation 4235 S. Memorial Drive Tulsa, OK 74145	J		x						x			x	x
Educational Dimensions Group Box 126 Stamford, CT 06904	J-S	x	x		x				x	x	x	x	x
Educational Direction Inc 181 Post Road Westport, CT 06880	J-S		x	x	x				x			x	x
Educational Enrichment Materials 357 Adams Street Bedford Hills, NY 10507	J-S	x		x	x				x	x		x	x
Educational Filmstrips 1401 19th Street Huntsville, TX 77340	J-S	x	x	x	x		x		x	x	x	x	x
Educational Images Box 367 Lyons Falls, NY 13368	J-S	x										x	x

Name & Address	Grade Range	the arts	education	home economics	humanities	industrial/vocational ed	languages	library science/media	mathematics	music/performing arts	physical education/sports	science	social sciences
Educational Materials & Equipment Company Box 17 Pelham, NY 10803	J-S											x	
Educational Media Inc 115 E. Fourth Street Ellensburg, WA 98926	J-S								x			x	
Educational Research Inc 4021 Greenwood Road Shreveport, LA 71109	J-S		x						x				
Educational Services Inc 1730 Eye Street, NW Washington, DC 20006	S						x						
Educational Technology Publications Inc 140 Sylvan Avenue Englewood Cliffs, NJ 07632	J-S		x										
H M Edwards 1931 S. Newport Street Denver, CO 80224	J-S		x				x			x			
Herbert M Elkins Company 10031 Commerce Avenue Tujunga, CA 91042	J-S	x			x				x			x	x
EMC Corporation 180 E. Sixth Street St. Paul, MN 55101	J-S		x		x	x	x		x		x	x	x
Encore Visual Education Inc 1235 S. Victory Boulevard Burbank, CA 91502	J-S	x	x	x	x		x					x	x
Encyclopaedia Britannica Educational Corporation 425 N. Michigan Avenue Chicago, IL 60611	J-S	x	x		x		x		x		x	x	x
English Language Services 16250 Ventura Boulevard Encino, CA 91436	S						x						

Name & Address	Grade Range	the arts	education	home economics	humanities	industrial/vocational ed	languages	library science/media	mathematics	music/performing arts	physical education/sports	science	social sciences
Enrichment Materials Inc 50 W. 44th Street New York, NY 10036	J		x	x	x	x							x
Enrichment Reading Corporation of America 102 E. North Street Iron Ridge, WI 53035	J								x		x	x	x
Entelek High Street Portsmouth, NH 03801	J-S		x						x				
Environmental Communications 62 Windward Avenue Venice, CA 90291	J-S	x										x	x
E S E Audiovisual 940 W. 22nd Street Hialeah, FL 33010	J-S	x	x	x								x	
European Art Color Slides 120 W. 70th Street New York, NY 10023	S	x										x	
Everett/Edwards Inc Box 1060 DeLand, FL 32720	S				x								x
Evinrude Motors 4143 North 27th Street, NE Milwaukee, WI 53216	S										x		
Eye Gate Media Inc 146-01 Archer Avenue Jamaica, NY 11435	J-S		x	x	x	x	x	x	x	x	x	x	x
Martin Ezra & Associates 45 Fairview Avenue Lansdowne, PA 19050	J-S	x	x							x		x	x
Fairchild Visuals 7 E. 12th Street New York, NY 10003	S		x	x									

Name & Address	Grade Range	the arts	education	home economics	humanities	industrial/vocational ed	languages	library science/media	mathematics	music/performing arts	physical education/sports	science	social sciences
Edward Feil Productions 4614 Prospect Avenue Cleveland, OH 44103	J-S				x							x	
Fellowship of Christian Athletes 812 Traders National Bank Bldg. 1125 Grand Kansas City, MO 64106	J-S										x		
Fenwick Productions 134 Steele Road West Hartford, CT 06119	J-S				x							x	
The Fideler Company 31 Ottawa NW Grand Rapids, MI 49502	J												x
Film Communicators 11136 Weddington Street North Hollywood, CA 91601	J-S		x	x			x					x	x
Film Modules Inc 172 Sullivan Street New York, NY 10012	J-S		x										
Film for the Humanities Inc Box 2053 Princeton, NJ 08540	J-S	x			x		x			x		x	x
Filmfair Communications 10820 Ventura Boulevard Studio City, CA 91604	J-S	x	x	x	x		x		x	x	x	x	x
Films of India Box 48303 Los Angeles, CA 90048	J-S	x			x					x			x
Fine Arts Films Inc 11632 Ventura Boulevard Studio City, CA 91604	J-S	x	x							x		x	x
Stuart Finley Inc 3428 Mansfield Road Falls Church, VA 22041	J-S		x									x	x

Name & Address	Grade Range	the arts	education	home economics	humanities	industrial/vocational ed	languages	library science/media	mathematics	music/performing arts	physical education/sports	science	social sciences
Fire Pretention through Films Inc Box 11 Newton Highlands, MA 02161	J-S		x										
Firebird Films 137 Carpenter Avenue Sea Cliff, NY 11579	J-S	x	x		x					x			x
Folkcraft Publishing Co Inc 10 Fenwick Street Newark, NJ 07114	J-S		x							x			
Folkways Records & Services Corp 43 W. 61st Street New York, NY 10023	J-S				x		x			x		x	x
Follett Publishing Company 1010 W. Washington Boulevard Chicago, IL 60607	J-S		x	x							x		x
Fordham Equipment & Publishing Company 3308 Edson Avenue Bronx, NY 10469	J-S	x	x	x	x				x		x	x	x
Franciscan Communications Center 1229 S. Santee Street Los Angeles, CA 90015	J-S		x		x								x
Gene Friedman Box 275 Wainscott, NY 11975	S	x			x					x			x
Friendship Press 475 Riverside Drive New York, NY 10027	J-S												x
Frith Films Box 424 Carmel Valley, CA 93924	J				x		x						x
GAF Corporation 140 W. 51st Street New York, NY 10020	J-S	x	x	x	x				x			x	x

Name & Address	Grade Range	the arts	education	home economics	humanities	industrial/vocational ed	languages	library science/media	mathematics	music/performing arts	physical education/sports	science	social sciences
Garret Park Press Garrett Park, MD 20766	J-S		x					x					
Girl Scouts of the USA 830 Third Avenue New York, NY 10022	J-S	x	x				x						x
Goldsmith's Music Shop Inc Audio Visual Dept. 301 E. Shore Road Great Neck, NY 11023	J-S						x			x		x	x
Graphic Curriculum Inc 699 Madison Avenue New York, NY 10021	J-S	x	x	x	x							x	x
Great American Film Factory Box 160281 Sacramento, CA 95816	J-S				x						x	x	x
Green Mountain Post Films Box 177 Montague, MA 01351	J-S				x					x		x	x
Greenwood Press Inc 51 Riverside Avenue Westport, CT 06880	J-S												x
Grolier Educational Corporation Old Sherman Turnpike Danbury, CT 06816	J-S								x				x
Grossman Publishers Inc 625 Madison Avenue New York, NY 10022	J-S		x		x	x					x	x	x
Guidance Associates Inc 757 Third Avenue New York, NY 10017	J-S		x	x	x					x		x	x
Hammond Inc 515 Valley Street Maplewood, NJ 07040	J-S		x								x	x	x

Name & Address	Grade Range	the arts	education	home economics	humanities	industrial/vocational ed	languages	library science/media	mathematics	music/performing arts	physical education/sports	science	social sciences
Handel Film Corporation 8730 Sunset Boulevard Los Angeles, CA 90069	J-S	x	x	x	x							x	x
Harcourt Brace Jovanovich Films 1001 Polk Street San Francisco, CA 94109	J-S	x	x		x	x		x	x			x	x
Harper & Row Publishers 10 E. 53rd Street New York, NY 10022	S		x		x			x				x	x
Harris County Center for the Retarded Inc Box 13403 Houston, TX 77019	Special		x										
Hartley Film Foundation Inc Cat Rock Road Cos Cob, CT 06807	J-S				x							x	
Harvard University Press 79 Garden Street Cambridge, MA 02138	S	x			x							x	
Harvest Educational Labs 73 Pelham Street Newport, RI 02840	J-S		x										
Harwyn Medical Photographers 1001 City Avenue, Suite 981 WB Philadelphia, PA 19151	S										x		
Hayden Book Co Inc 50 Essex Street Rochelle Park, NJ 07662	J-S								x			x	x
Hayes Publishing Co Inc 6340 Hamilton Avenue Cincinnati, OH 45224	J-S		x										x
Hayes School Publishing Co Inc 321 Pennwood Avenue Wilkinsburg, PA 15221	J-S		x						x				x

Name & Address	Grade Range	the arts	education	home economics	humanities	industrial/vocational ed	languages	library science/media	mathematics	music/performing arts	physical education/sports	science	social sciences
D C Heath & Company 125 Spring Street Lexington, MA 02173	J-S						x	x				x	x
Stuart Hersh Productions 680 Fifth Avenue New York, NY 10019	J-S	x	x		x					x	x	x	x
J E G Hess Productions 217½ Second Avenue New York, NY 10003	J-S	x	x		x					x			x
Hester & Associates 11422 Hines Boulevard Dallas, TX 75229	J-S	x		x				x			x		
Alfred Higgins Productions 9100 Sunset Boulevard Los Angeles, CA 90069	J-S										x		x
Hoffman Electronics Corporation 4423 Arden Drive El Monte, CA 91734	J-S		x										
Hoffman Occupational Learning Systems Division 4423 Arden Drive El Monte, CA 91734	J-S		x			x							
Theodore Holcomb Films 11 E. 90th Street New York, NY 10028	J-S												x
Holt, Rinehart & Winston School Department 383 Madison Avenue New York, NY 10017	J-S				x	x			x			x	x
Houghton Mifflin Company Media Department One Beacon Street Boston, MA 02107	J-S	x	x	x	x		x		x			x	x
Hubbard Scientific Company Box 105 Northbrook, IL 60062	J-S		x								x	x	x

Name & Address	Grade Range	the arts	education	home economics	humanities	industrial/vocational ed	languages	library science/media	mathematics	music/performing arts	physical education/sports	science	social sciences
Ideal School Supply Company 11000 S. Lavergne Avenue Oak Lawn, IL 60453	J-S			x					x		x		
Image Associates Box 40106 352 Conejo Road Santa Barbara, CA 93103	J-S	x	x		x						x	x	x
Impact Films 144 Bleecker Street New York, NY 10012	J-S											x	
Imperial Educational Resources 19 Marble Avenue Pleasantville, NY 10570	J-S	x	x	x	x				x	x	x	x	x
Imperial International Learning Box 548 Kankakee, IL 60901	J								x		x	x	x
Indian House Box 472 Taos, NM 87571	J-S									x		x	
Instructional Aids Inc Box 191 Mankato, MN 56001	J		x								x	x	x
Instructional/Communications Technology Inc 10 Stepar Place Huntington Station, NY 11746	J-S				x								
Instructional Dynamics Inc 666 N. Lake Drive Chicago, IL 60611	J-S		x	x					x		x	x	x
Instructo/McGraw-Hill Paoli, PA 19301	J		x						x			x	x
Instrument Society of America 400 Stanwix Street Pittsburgh, PA 15222	S		x									x	

Name & Address	Grade Range	the arts	education	home economics	humanities	industrial/vocational ed	languages	library science/media	mathematics	music/performing arts	physical education/sports	science	social sciences
Integrative Learning Systems Inc 140 N. Maryland Avenue Glendale, CA 91206	J-S		x		x	x							
Interculture Associates Box 277 Thompson, CT 06277	J-S	x	x		x								x
International Film Bureau Inc 332 S. Michigan Avenue Chicago, IL 60604	J-S	x			x								x
International Film Foundations Inc 475 Fifth Avenue, Room 916 New York, NY 10017	J-S												x
International Motion Pictures Ltd Box 3201 Erie, PA 16512	J-S	x			x								x
Intext/Driver Testing Equipment Division Pawnee & Oak Scranton, PA 18515	S		x										
IQ Films Inc One Maxwell Place Wappingers Falls, NY 12590	S												x
Jabberwocky 4 Commercial Boulevard Novato, CA 94947	J-S								x		x		
Joint Council on Economic Education 1212 Avenue of the Americas New York, NY 10036	J-S			x									x
Kalmbach Publishing Company 1027 N. Seventh Street Milwaukee, WI 53233	J-S			x									
Kauffman & Boyce Productions Box 283 Allston, MA 02134	J-S	x	x		x								x

Name & Address	Grade Range	the arts	education	home economics	humanities	industrial/vocational ed	languages	library science/media	mathematics	music/performing arts	physical education/sports	science	social sciences
Killiam Shows Inc 6 E. 39th Street New York, NY 10016	S	x								x	x		x
Walter J Klein Co Ltd 6301 Carmel Road Charlotte, NC 28211	J-S		x										
Lab-Volt Ltd 5368 13th Avenue Rosemont, Quebec H1X 2X8, Canada	J-S		x									x	
Lansford Publishing Co Inc 1088 Lincoln Avenue Box 8711 San Jose, CA 95155	S	x	x		x							x	x
Marjorie S Larsen 1754 Middlefield Stockton, CA 95204	J-S									x			
Lawren Productions Inc Box 666 Mendocino, CA 95460	J-S	x	x	x						x			x
Learning & Information Inc 315 Central Park W. New York, NY 10025	J-S		x	x	x							x	
Learning Corporation of America 1350 Avenue of the Americas New York, NY 10019	J-S	x	x		x		x			x	x	x	x
Learning through Seeing Inc LTS Building, Box 368 Sunland, CA 91040	J-S		x						x				
Learning Tree Filmstrips 934 Pearl Street Boulder, CO 80302	J		x	x					x	x		x	x
Learning Ventures 666 Fifth Avenue New York, NY 10019	J-S		x		x								x

Name & Address	Grade Range	the arts	education	home economics	humanities	industrial/vocational ed	languages	library science/media	mathematics	music/performing arts	physical education/sports	science	social sciences
Walter Lewisohn Associates Route 1, Box 284 Yorktown Heights, NY 10598	J-S	x	x	x						x			
Peter Li Inc/Pflaum Press 2451 E. River Road Dayton, OH 45439	J-S		x										
Library Filmstrip Center 3033 Aloma Wichita, KS 67211	J-S	x	x	x	x							x	x
Library of Congress Recorded Sound Section Music Division Washington, DC 20540	J-S	x			x					x			x
Lincoln Electric Company 22801 St. Clair Avenue Cleveland, OH 44117	S		x										
J B Lippincott Educational Publishing Division East Washington Square Philadelphia, PA 19105	J-S											x	x
Listening Library Inc One Park Avenue Old Greenwich, CT 06870	J-S	x	x		x		x		x	x		x	x
The Little Red Filmhouse 666 N. Robertson Los Angeles, CA 90069	J-S	x	x									x	
Lohmann Films 1006 Sunset Court West Lafayette, IN 47906	J-S	x			x							x	x
Hubert A Lowman Route 1, Box 110 Arroyo Grande, CA 93420	J											x	x
Lutheran Film Associates 360 Park Avenue S. New York, NY 10010	S											x	

Name & Address	Grade Range	the arts	education	home economics	humanities	industrial/vocational ed	languages	library science/media	mathematics	music/performing arts	physical education/sports	science	social sciences
Lyceum Productions Inc Box 1226 Laguna Beach, CA 92652	J-S				x							x	x
Macmillan Films Inc 34 MacQuesten Parkway S. Mount Vernon, NY 10550	J-S	x	x	x	x				x	x	x	x	x
Marsh Film Enterprises Inc Box 8082 Shawnee Mission, KS 66208	J		x	x			x				x	x	x
Mass Communications Inc 25 Sylvan Road S. Westport, CT 06880	S	x	x		x								x
Mast Development Company 2212 E. 12th Street Davenport, IA 52803	J-S								x		x		
McGraw-Hill Book Company 1221 Avenue of the Americas New York, NY 10020	J-S	x	x	x	x				x	x		x	x
McKnight Publishing Company Box 2854 Bloomington, IL 61701	J-S	x		x									
McMahon Electronic Engineering 381 W. Seventh Street San Pedro, CA 90731	J-S		x						x				
Media Materials Inc Remington Avenue Baltimore, MD 21210	J-S		x						x			x	x
Media Research & Development Arizona State University Tempe, AZ 85281	J-S		x					x					
Media Research Associates Inc 1712 S.E. 23rd Street Salem, OR 97302	J		x						x				

Name & Address	Grade Range	Subject Areas											
		the arts	education	home economics	humanities	industrial/vocational ed	languages	library science/media	mathematics	music/performing arts	physical education/sports	science	social sciences
Media Resources Center Iowa State University Ames, IA 50011	S		x	x						x		x	
Media Systems Inc 3637 E. 7800 S. Salt Lake City, UT 84121	J-S							x					
Medical Plastics Laboratory Inc Box 38 Gatesville, TX 76528	J-S											x	
Memorex Corporation 1200 Memorex Drive Santa Clara, CA 95052	J-S		x										
Mental Health Training Film Program Harvard Medical School 58 Fenwood Road Boston, MA 02115	S		x		x					x		x	
Charles E Merrill Publishing 1300 Alum Creek Drive Columbus, OH 43216	J-S		x						x			x	x
Metropolitan Pittsburgh Public Broadcasting Inc 4802 Fifth Avenue Pittsburgh, PA 15213	J-S		x									x	
Micom Ltd 3405 W. Chester Pike Newtown Square, PA 19073	J-S	x	x	x	x	x			x		x	x	x
Micro Photo Division Bell & Howell Old Mansfield Road Wooster, OH 44691	J-S	x	x	x	x	x			x		x	x	x
Midwest Visuals Inc Box 38 Brimson, MN 55602	J-S			x	x							x	x

Name & Address	Grade Range	the arts	education	home economics	humanities	industrial/vocational ed	languages	library science/media	mathematics	music/performing arts	physical education/sports	science	social sciences
Milady Publishing Corporation 3839 White Plains Road Bronx, NY 10467	J-S		x	x									
Mark Miller Isley Road Santa Barbara, CA 93101	J-S												x
Miller Productions Inc 800 West Avenue, Box 5584 Austin, TX 78763	J-S		x		x								
Milliken Publishing Company 1100 Research Boulevard St. Louis, MO 63132	J-S		x				x		x			x	x
Mini Productions Inc 725 Liberty Avenue Pittsburgh, PA 15222	J-S		x										
MMI Corporation 2950 Wyman Parkway Baltimore, MD	S											x	
Modern Education Systems Inc 524 E. Jackson Street Goshen, IN 46526	J-S												x
Arthur Mokin Productions Inc 17 W. 60th Street New York, NY 10023	J-S	x	x	x	x						x	x	x
Monitor Recordings Inc 156 Fifth Avenue New York, NY 10010	J-S	x					x			x			
Montage Films 924 Garden Street, Bldg G Santa Barbara, CA 93101	J-S				x					x		x	x
Moody Institute of Science 12000 E. Washington Blvd. Whittier, CA 90606	J-S								x			x	x

Name & Address	Grade Range	the arts	education	home economics	humanities	industrial/vocational ed	languages	library science/media	mathematics	music/performing arts	physical education/sports	science	social sciences
Moonlight Productions 2650 California Street Mountain View, CA 94040	J-S											x	
The Thomas More Association 180 N. Wabash Avenue Chicago, IL 60601	S												x
Mosaic Media Inc 413 Cottage Avenue Glen Ellyn, IL 60137	J-S								x				
MRC Films 71 W. 23rd Street New York, NY 10010	J-S								x			x	x
Multi-Media Productions Inc Box 5097 Stanford, CA 94305	J-S		x	x					x			x	x
Musilog Corporation Box 1199, 1600 Anacapa Santa Barbara, CA 93102	J-S	x								x			
National Aeronautics & Space Administration Code FAM Washington, DC 20546	J-S											x	
National Association of Hearing & Speech Agencies Thayer Avenue Silver Spring, MD 20910	S		x										
National Career Consultants Inc 1300 E. Arapaho Road Richardson, TX 75081	J-S		x			x							
National Cathedral Association Washington Cathedral Mount St. Alban Washington, DC 20016	J-S	x	x										
National Dairy Council Division of Education 6300 N. River Road Rosemont, IL 60018	J-S			x								x	x

Name & Address	Grade Range	the arts	education	home economics	humanities	industrial/vocational ed	languages	library science/media	mathematics	music/performing arts	physical education/sports	science	social sciences
National Education Association 1201 16th Street, NW Washington, DC 20036	J-S		x										
National Educational Media Inc 15760 Ventura Boulevard Encino, CA 91436	J-S		x	x									x
National Federation Sports Film Federation Place Elgin, IL 60120	J-S										x		
National Film Board of Canada 1251 Avenue of the Americas New York, NY 10020	J-S	x	x	x	x				x	x	x	x	x
National Gallery of Art-Extension Service Constitution Avenue at Sixth, NW Washington, DC 20565	J-S	x											x
National Geographic Society 17th & M Streets, NW Washington, DC 20036	J-S											x	x
National Golf Foundation 200 Castlewood Drive North Palm Beach, FL 33408	J-S												x
National Livestock & Meat Board 444 N. Michigan Avenue Chicago, IL 60611	J-S			x									x
National Teaching Aids Inc 120 Fulton Avenue Garden City Park, NY 11040	J-S											x	
Nauman Films Inc Box 232 Custer, SD 57730	J-S	x	x	x	x	x				x	x	x	x
Nelson Gallery-Atkins Museum 4525 Oak Street Kansas City, MO 64111	J-S	x											

Name & Address	Grade Range	the arts	education	home economics	humanities	industrial/vocational ed	languages	library science/media	mathematics	music/performing arts	physical education/sports	science	social sciences
New Century Education Corporation 275 Old New Brunswick Road Piscataway, NJ 08854	J	x											
New Day Films Box 315 Franklin Lakes, NJ 07471	J-S	x	x	x									x
New Film Company 331 Newbury Street Boston, MA 02115	J-S	x	x		x					x		x	x
New York Graphic Society Ltd 140 Greenwich Avenue Greenwich, CT 06830	J-S	x											x
New York State Colleges of Agriculture & Life Sciences & Human Ecology, Cornell University, Media Services 201 Roberts Hall, Cornell Univ. Ithaca, NY 14853	J-S		x	x								x	x
9200 Film Center Box 1113 Minneapolis, MN 55440	J-S		x	x						x			
Noble & Noble Publishers Inc One Dag Hammarskjold Plaza New York, NY 10017	J-S		x										x
Northern Illinois University Altgeld Hall, Room 116 DeKalb, IL 60115	S		x	x									x
Northwest Media Associates 158 Thomas Street Seattle, WA 98109	J-S		x	x									
Jeffrey Norton Publishers Inc 145 E. 49th Street New York, NY 10017	S	x	x	x	x					x	x	x	x

Name & Address	Grade Range	the arts	education	home economics	humanities	industrial/vocational ed	languages	library science/media	mathematics	music/performing arts	physical education/sports	science	social sciences
Nystrom 3333 Elston Avenue Chicago, IL 60618	J-S		x									x	x
Odeon Films Inc Box 315 Franklin Lakes, NJ 07417	S		x									x	
Office for Educational Practice University of Guelph Guelph, Ontario N1G 2W1, Canada	S		x	x						x		x	x
Ohio Historical Society Ohio Historical Center Columbus, OH 43211	J-S												x
Olympus Publishing Company 1760 E. 1300 S. Salt Lake City, UT 84105	J-S	x	x										
Organization of American States Pan America Building 17th Street & Constitution Avenue Washington, DC 20006	J-S	x					x						
Outdoor Pictures Box 277 Anacortes, WA 98221	J-S	x	x	x	x				x			x	x
Pacific Records Company Box 26306 800 S. Fenton Street Denver, CO 80226	J-S									x			
Panoramic Teaching Aids Inc 1810 Rapids Avenue Alexandria, LA 71301	J-S		x						x			x	x
Paramount Communications 5451 Marathon Street Hollywood, CA 90038	J-S	x	x	x	x	x			x	x	x	x	x
Parents' Magazine Films Inc 52 Vanderbilt Avenue New York, NY 10017	J-S		x	x	x								x

Name & Address	Grade Range	the arts	education	home economics	humanities	industrial/vocational ed	languages	library science/media	mathematics	music/performing arts	physical education/sports	science	social sciences
Parthenon Pictures 2625 Temple Street Los Angeles, CA 90026	J-S												X
Pathe News Inc/Pathe Pictures Inc 250 W. 57th Street New York, NY 10019	J-S		X		X						X		X
Pathescope Educational Media Inc 71 Weyman Avenue New Rochelle, NY 10802	J-S		X				X	X					X
Pathways of Sound Inc 102 Mt. Auburn Street Cambridge, MA 02138	J-S	X	X				X			X			
Pergamon Press Inc Maxwell House Elmsford, NY 10523	S				X							X	X
Perkins School for the Blind Watertown, MA 02172	J-S		X										
The Petersen Company 1330 N. Vine Street Hollywood, CA 90028	J-S										X		
Petite Film Company 708 N. 62nd Street Seattle, WA 98103	J-S	X										X	X
Photo Arts Company RD 4 Manheim, PA 17545	J-S	X		X									X
Photo Lab Inc 3825 Georgie Avenue, NW Washington, DC 20011	J-S	X		X									X
Pictura Films 111 Eighth Avenue New York, NY 10011	J-S	X	X	X	X		X		X	X			X
Pied Piper Production Box 320 Verdugo City, CA 91046	J-S								X				X

Name & Address	Grade Range	the arts	education	home economics	humanities	industrial/vocational ed	languages	library science/media	mathematics	music/performing arts	physical education/sports	science	social sciences
Pittaro Productions RD 1 Old Castle Point Road Wappingers Falls, NY 12590	J-S	x								x	x		
Playette Corporation 301 E. Shore Road Great Neck, NY 11023	J-S	x					x						x
The Plough Publishing House Rifton, NY 12471	J-S									x			x
Point Lobos Productions 20417 Califa Street Woodland Hills, CA 91367	J-S	x					x			x		x	x
Polymorph Films Inc 331 Newbury Street Boston, MA 02115	S			x	x								x
Pomfret House Route 44 Pomfret Center, CT 06259	J-S				x	x					x	x	x
Portafilms Inc 4180 Dixie Highway Drayton Plains, MI 48020	J-S	x	x										x
Prentice-Hall Media Inc 150 White Plains Road Tarrytown, NY 10591	J-S	x	x	x	x		x		x	x		x	x
Prentice-Hall of Canada Limited 1870 Birchmount Road Scarborough, Ontario M1P 2J7, Canada	J-S	x	x	x	x		x					x	x
Howard Preston Films 920 Centinela Avenue Santa Monica, CA 90403	S											x	
Professional Arts Inc Box 8003 Stanford, CA 94305	S		x										x

Name & Address	Grade Range	the arts	education	home economics	humanities	industrial/vocational ed	languages	library science/media	mathematics	music/performing arts	physical education/sports	science	social sciences
Prothmann Associates Inc 650 Thomas Avenue Baldwin, NY 11510	J-S	x			x							x	x
Psychotechnics Inc 1900 Pickwick Avenue Glenview, IL 60025	J-S		x										
Purpose Film Center 2625 Temple Street Los Angeles, CA 90026	J-S		x								x		
Pyramid Films 2801 Colorado, Box 1048 Santa Monica, CA 90406	J-S	x	x	x	x		x	x	x	x		x	x
Q-Ed Productions Inc 2282 Towns Gate Road Westlake Village, CA 91360	J		x						x			x	x
Radio & TV Commission of the Southern Baptist Convention 6350 W. Freeway Fort Worth, TX 76150	J-S	x			x							x	x
Ramic Productions 4911 Birch Street Newport Beach, CA 92660	J-S		x										
Ramsgate Films 704 Santa Monica Boulevard Santa Monica, CA 90401	J-S		x	x					x		x	x	x
Rand McNally & Company Box 7600 Chicago, IL 60680	J-S		x			x	x		x			x	x
Random House Miller-Brody Productions Inc 400 Hahn Road Westminster, MD 21157	J-S	x	x		x		x	x	x			x	x
Conrad Calvin Rankin Enterprises Box 25 Burlingame, CA 94010	J-S		x										

Name & Address	Grade Range	the arts	education	home economics	humanities	industrial/vocational ed	languages	library science/media	mathematics	music/performing arts	physical education/sports	science	social sciences
RCA Music Service Educational Department 6550 E. 30th Street Indianapolis, IN 46291	J						x			x			
The Reading Laboratory Inc Marshall Street South Norwalk, CT 06854	J-S		x	x	x						x	x	x
Recording for the Blind Inc 215 E. 28th Street New York, NY 10022	J-S	x	x	x	x	x		x	x			x	x
Rediscovery Productions Inc 2 Half Mile Common Westport, CT 06880	J-S		x										
Regents Publishing Co Inc 2 Park Avenue New York, NY 10016	J-S						x						
REM Productions Box 10207 Riviera Beach, FL 33404	S								x		x		
Rhythms Productions Whitney Building, Box 34485 Los Angeles, CA 90034	J-S		x							x			
Richter McBride Productions Inc 150 E. 52nd Street New York, NY 10022	J-S		x		x				x	x		x	x
RMI Media Productions Inc 120 W. 72nd Street Kansas City, MO 64114	J-S	x	x	x	x				x	x	x	x	x
ROA Films 1696 N. Astor Street Milwaukee, WI 53202	J-S		x		x					x	x		x
William H Sadlier Inc 11 Park Place New York, NY 10007	J-S		x										x

Name & Address	Grade Range	the arts	education	home economics	humanities	industrial/vocational ed	languages	library science/media	mathematics	music/performing arts	physical education/sports	science	social sciences
Sandler Institutional Films Inc Mel Road Hollywood, CA 90046	J-S		x										x
Alan Sands Productions 565 Fifth Avenue New York, NY 10017	J-S											x	
S C Educational Television Commission 2712 Millwood Avenue Columbia, SC 29205	J-S	x	x	x	x		x			x		x	x
Scala Fine Arts Publishers Inc 343 Madison Avenue New York, NY 10036	J-S	x			x								
William Schlottmann Productions 536 E. Fifth Street, Suite 18 New York, NY 10009	J-S		x										
Scholar's Choice Ltd 50 Ballantyne Avenue Stratford, Ontario N5A 6T9, Canada	J	x							x	x	x	x	x
Scholastic Magazines Inc 50 W. 44th Street New York, NY 10036	J-S		x	x	x				x	x	x	x	
Science & Mankind Inc Communications Park, Box 200 White Plains, NY 10602	J-S		x						x	x			
Science Media Box 910 Boca Raton, FL 33432	S		x								x		
Science Related Materials Box 1422 Janesville, WI 53545	S										x		
Science Research Associates Inc 155 N. Wacker Drive Chicago, IL 60606	J-S		x										

Name & Address	Grade Range	the arts	education	home economics	humanities	industrial/vocational ed	languages	library science/media	mathematics	music/performing arts	physical education/sports	science	social sciences
Science Software Systems Inc 11899 W. Pico Boulevard W. Los Angeles, CA 90064	J-S		x	x								x	
Scientificom 708 N. Dearborn Avenue Chicago, IL 60610	S		x										
Scope Productions Inc Box 5515 Fresno, CA 93755	J-S		x	x						x	x	x	x
Screen Education Enterprises Inc Box C-19126 Seattle, WA 98109	J-S												x
Screenscope Inc 1022 Wilson Boulevard, Suite 2000 Arlington, VA 22209	J-S	x	x	x	x		x			x		x	x
Dale E Shaffer, Library Consultant 437 Jennings Avenue Salem, OH 44460	J-S		x		x		x						x
Shell Oil Company Film Division One Shell Plaza, Box 2463 Houston, TX 77001	J-S		x								x	x	x
Shimbal Studios Box 313 Flushing, NY 11367	J-S	x			x								x
Shorewood Reproductions Inc 475 Tenth Avenue New York, NY 10018	J-S	x											
Silo Cinema Inc Box 7, Canal Street Station New York, NY 10013	J-S				x								x
Silver Burdett Company 250 James Street Morristown, NJ 07690	J-S			x	x					x		x	x

Name & Address	Grade Range	the arts	education	home economics	humanities	industrial/vocational ed	languages	library science/media	mathematics	music/performing arts	physical education/sports	science	social sciences
Simile II 218 12th Street, Box 910 Del Mar, CA 92014	J-S												x
S-L Film Productions Box 41108 Los Angeles, CA 90041	J-S	x	x		x				x	x	x	x	x
Sleeping Giant Films Inc 3019 Dixwell Avenue Hamden, CT 06518	J-S	x	x				x						x
Smithsonian Institution Office of Printing & Photographic Services Washington, DC 20560	J-S	x			x	x					x		x
Bill Snyder Films Inc 1419 First Avenue South Box 2784 Fargo, ND 58108	J-S	x				x							
The Society for Nutrition Education 2140 Shattuck Avenue, Suite 1110 Berkeley, CA 94704	S			x									
Society for Visual Education Inc 1345 Diversey Parkway Chicago, IL 60614	J-S		x	x	x				x		x	x	x
Soundings 2150 Concord Boulevard Concord, CA 94520	J-S	x	x		x					x			x
Soundwords Inc 56-11 214 Street Bayside, NY 11364	S		x	x									
Spenco Medical Corporation Box 8113 Waco, TX 76710	J-S		x								x		
Spoken Arts Inc 310 North Avenue New Rochelle, NY 10801	J-S	x			x		x		x				

Name & Address	Grade Range	the arts	education	home economics	humanities	industrial/vocational ed	languages	library science/media	mathematics	music/performing arts	physical education/sports	science	social sciences
Spoken Language Services Inc Box 783 Ithaca, NY 14850	J-S						x						
Stanton Films 2417 Artesia Boulevard Redondo Beach, CA 90278	J-S						x				x	x	x
H M Stone Productions Inc 6 E. 45th Street New York, NY 10017	J-S	x	x	x	x			x	x			x	x
Marty Stouffer Productions Ltd 300 S. Spring Street Aspen, CO 81611	S											x	x
Sunburst Communications 39-41 Washington Avenue Pleasantville, NY 10570	J-S		x	x	x							x	x
Teaching Aids Inc Box 1798 Costa Mesa, CA 92626	S			x	x								
Tel-a-Train Inc 3661 Brainerd Road, Suite 208 Chattanooga, TN 37411	S										x		
Telekinetics 1229 S. Santee Street Los Angeles, CA 90015	J-S		x		x								x
Telstar Productions Inc 366 N. Prior Avenue St. Paul, MN 55104	S								x			x	x
Texture Films Inc 1600 Broadway New York, NY 10019	J-S	x	x		x		x			x	x	x	x
Thorne Films Inc 934 Pearl Boulder, CO 80302	J-S	x				x						x	x

Name & Address	Grade Range	the arts	education	home economics	humanities	industrial/vocational ed	languages	library science/media	mathematics	music/performing arts	physical education/sports	science	social sciences
Time-Life Films Multimedia Division 100 Eisenhower Drive Paramus, NJ 07652	J-S	x	x		x		x		x	x	x	x	x
Track & Field News Box 296 Los Altos, CA 94022	S										x		
Troll Associates 320 Route 17 Mahwah, NJ 07430	J-S		x	x	x			x		x		x	x
Union of American Hebrew Congregations 838 Fifth Avenue New York, NY 10021	J-S		x										
Unitarian Universalist Association Department of Education & Social Concern 25 Beacon Street Boston, MA 02173	J-S		x										x
United Church Press/Pilgrim Press 1505 Race Street Philadelphia, PA 19102	J-S		x										
United Learning 6633 W. Howard Street Niles, IL 60648	J-S		x	x	x			x			x	x	
United Methodist Communications 1525 McGavock Street Nashville, TN 37203	J-S					x							x
United Nations, Radio & Visual Services United Nations New York, NY 10017	J-S	x									x	x	
United States History Society Inc 8154 Ridgeway Skokie, IL 60076	J-S												x

Name & Address	Grade Range	the arts	education	home economics	humanities	industrial/vocational ed	languages	library science/media	mathematics	music/performing arts	physical education/sports	science	social sciences
United States Publishers Association Inc 46 Lafayette Avenue New Rochelle, NY 10801	J-S												x
United Synagogue of America 155 Fifth Avenue New York, NY 10010	J-S						x						
United Transparencies Inc Box 688 Binghamton, NY 13902	J-S		x	x	x		x	x				x	x
University of Arizona Microcampus Tucson, AZ 85721	S								x			x	x
University of California Broadcast Production & Media Services University Park Los Angeles, CA 90007	S		x		x					x		x	
University of Iowa Audiovisual Center C215 East Hall Iowa City, IA 52242	J-S	x	x		x					x		x	x
University of Missouri-Columbia 505 E. Stewart Road Columbia, MO 65211	J-S	x	x	x	x		x		x	x	x	x	x
University of Washington Press Seattle, WA 98105	S	x	x										x
University Prints 21 East Street Winchester, MA 01890	S	x			x								
Unusual Films Bob Jones University Greenville, SC 29614	S	x								x			
US Committee for Unicef 331 E. 38th Street New York, NY 10017	J-S												x

Name & Address	Grade Range	the arts	education	home economics	humanities	industrial/vocational ed	languages	library science/media	mathematics	music/performing arts	physical education/sports	science	social sciences
US Navy Office of Information Production Service Division Pentagon, Room 2D340 Washington, DC 20350	S		x									x	x
VWR Scientific Company 260 Needham Street Newton, MA 02164	S											x	
Van Nostrand Reinhold Company 135 W. 50th Street, 13th Floor New York, NY 10020	J-S	x	x	x									
Vedo Films 85 Longview Road Port Washington, NY 11050	J-S									x			x
Viking Penguin Inc 625 Madison Avenue New York, NY 10022	J-S	x	x		x							x	x
Virginia State Department of Education Film Production Service, Box 6 Q Richmond, VA 23216	J-S		x									x	x
Visual Education Association 581 W. Leffel Lane, Box 1206 Springfield, OH 45506	S						x		x			x	x
Visual Education Corporation 14 Washington Road, Box 2321 Princeton, NJ 08540	J-S	x	x		x				x			x	
Visual Education Service Yale University Divinity School 409 Prospect Street New Haven, CT 06511	S	x	x		x								
Visual Instruction Productions 295 W. Fourth Street New York, NY 10014	J-S		x							x	x		
Visual Resources Inc 152 W. 42nd Street, No. 1219 New York, NY 10036	S	x			x					x			x

Name & Address	Grade Range	the arts	education	home economics	humanities	industrial/vocational ed	languages	library science/media	mathematics	music/performing arts	physical education/sports	science	social sciences
Vocational Education Productions California Polytechnic State Univ. San Luis Obispo, CA 93407	J-S		x			x						x	
Warner Bros Inc Non-Theatrical Division 4000 Warner Boulevard Burbank, CA 91522	S	x	x		x					x	x		x
Warner Educational Productions 10041 Beverly Drive Huntington Beach, CA 92646	J-S	x											
Wayne State University Film Library 5448 Cass Avenue Detroit, MI 48202	S	x	x	x	x		x		x	x	x	x	x
Weber Costello 1900 N. Narragansett Chicago, IL 60639	J		x						x		x		
West Virginia University Morgantown, WV 26505	J-S	x	x		x					x		x	x
Western Instruction Television Inc 1549 N. Vine Street Los Angeles, CA 90028	J									x		x	x
Westport Communications Group Inc 155 Post Road E. Westport, CT 06880	J-S	x	x	x	x				x	x	x	x	x
WFF'N Proof Learning Games Associates 1490-UO South Boulevard Ann Arbor, MI 48104	J-S		x						x			x	
Wilmac Recorders 301 E. Shore Road Great Neck, NY 11023	S					x							
H Wilson Corporation 555 W. Taft Drive South Holland, IL 60473	J-S		x									x	x

Name & Address	Grade Range	the arts	education	home economics	humanities	industrial/vocational ed	languages	library science/media	mathematics	music/performing arts	physical education/sports	science	social sciences
Windmills Ltd Production Box 5300 Santa Monica, CA 90405	J-S		x		x								x
World Future Society 4916 St. Elmo Avenue Washington, DC 20014	S	x	x		x					x		x	x
Xerox Education Publications/ Xerox Films 245 Long Hill Road Middletown, CT 06457	J-S		x	x	x	x		x		x		x	x
Yellow Ball Workshop 62 Tarbell Avenue Lexington, MA 02173	J-S	x			x					x			x
Your Health 5841 S. Maryland Avenue Chicago, IL 60637	J-S		x										
Zachry, Naill & Associates Inc Box 1739 Abilene, TX 79604	S											x	x
Zipporah Films Inc 54 Lewis Wharf Boston, MA 02110	J-S		x		x							x	x

INDEX